cool cards

edited by
David E. Carter

book design & captions by
Suzanna M.W. Brown

The Carter Library of Design

Cool Cards

First published 1998 by Hearst Books International
1350 Avenue of the Americas
New York, NY 10019

ISBN: 0688-16047-6

Distributed in the U.S. and Canada by
Watson-Guptill Publications
1515 Broadway
New York, NY 10036
Tel: 800-451-1741
           732-363-4511 in NJ, AK, HI
Fax: 732-363-0338

Distributed throughout the rest of the world by
Hearst Books International
1350 Avenue of the Americas
New York, NY 10019
Fax: 212-261-6795

First published in Germany by:
NIPPAN

Nippon Shuppan Hanbai
Deutschland GmbH
Krefelder Str. 85
D-40549 Dusseldorf
Tel: (0211)5048089
Fax: (0211)5049326

ISBN: 3-931884-22-8

Printed in Hong Kong by Everbest Printing Company
through Four Colour Imports, Louisville, Kentucky.

A lot of business cards have a precise "corporate" look.

You won't find any of these in **this** book.

What you will find are cards that are groovy, awesome, boss, hip, nifty, funky, solid, right-on, intense, and a lot of other adjectives.

You want to see nearly 400 cool cards? You've come to the right place.

NANCY K. WEIMER

Food Consultant

74 North Greenwood Avenue
Hopewell, New Jersey 08525

609-466-0481

Client   Nancy K. Weimer
              Hopewell, New Jersey
Design Firm   Janet Payne Graphic Designer
              Hopewell, New Jersey

The art for this food consultant's card "was created by inking and printing
a real 'live' dead fish! Very smelly, but the results are great."

Client   the Second Opinion
              Phoenix, Arizona
Design Firm   After Hours Creative
              Phoenix, Arizona

Reversed out of a rust color are the client's initials asking the question
"SO?" You flip the card to find out "So what?" and discover the client's
name, address, and numbers on the other side.

the Second Opinion, strategy, marketing & capital
Peter Juergens, Marketing Consultant
434 Marietta St., NW, Suite 302 Atlanta, GA 30313
e-mail address secondop@aol.com
phone 404.222.9822 fax 404.222.9427

Chris Warren
Concierge

444 Columbus Avenue
San Francisco, CA 94133

Tel: 415.433.9111
Fax: 415.362.6292

Email: HotelBoheme@
MCIMail.com

Joel Morgenstern

444 Columbus Avenue
San Francisco, CA 94133

Tel: 415.433.9111
Fax: 415.362.6292

Email: HotelBoheme@
MCIMail.com

Client   Hotel Bohéme
              San Francisco,
              California
Design Firm   A E R I A L
              San Francisco,
              California

Full-color cards, printed on both
sides with images indicative of
1950s Bohemia, make a strong
identity statement for this North
Beach hotel.

Bruce Abney
General Manager

444 Columbus Avenue
San Francisco, CA 94133

Tel: 415.433.9111
Fax: 415.362.6292

Email: HotelBoheme@
MCIMail.com

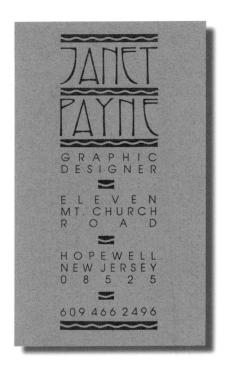

Client   Janet Payne Graphic Designer
              Hopewell, New Jersey
Design Firm Janet Payne Graphic Designer
              Hopewell, New Jersey

Blue-purple ink printed on green stock with blue-purple fibers adds a nice touch of unity to this business card. Interesting typography has a calligraphic feel.

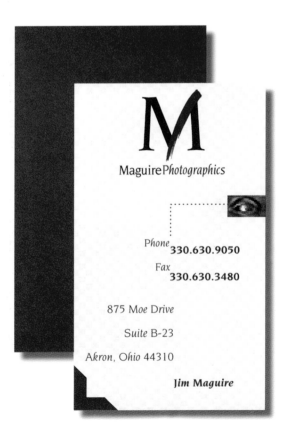

Client   Maguire Photographics
              Akron, Ohio
Design Firm Denise Kemper Design
              Wadsworth, Ohio

Rich purple printed full bleed on the back and as an accent color on the front makes these photographer's cards easy to recognize. A picture mount shape is placed in the bottom left corner. Typography techniques include using plain letters for capitals and italic letters for the remaining type.

DAVID KINGSBURY

PHOTOGRAPHY

4814 WASHINGTON AVENUE

ST LOUIS MISSOURI 63108

TELEPHONE 314 361 8081

FACSIMILE 314 361 1245

Client   David Kingsbury Photography
              St. Louis, Missouri
Design Firm   CUBE Advertising & Design
              St. Louis, Missouri

Bright green on purple create an almost complimentary color scheme for this photographer's card. Type is set in all caps while the icon is symbolic of both the profession and the professional's name.

Client   Dante's Restaurants Inc.
              State College, Pennsylvania
Design Firm   Sommese Design
              State College, Pennsylvania

The name of the president of this company (and his obvious good humor) make for a clever visual word play. The front of the business card includes a crosshatched drawing of a gorilla. Open the flap and the great ape is serving an elegant meal. The inside flap includes the client's name, address, etc. while the back of the card lists all restaurants associated with Dante's.

ANDY ZANGRILLI

President

DANTE'S RESTAURANTS, INC.

936 E. College Ave.

State College, PA 16801

814-234-1344

Fax 814-237-2925

ANDY ZANGORILLA

Client   Cranford Creations
              Grapevine, Texas
Design Firm   Wet Paper Bag Graphic Design
              Fort Worth, Texas

The solution to enhance this fiber artist's corporate identity causes
one to feel there could not have possibly been a better answer.
Fibers in the card stock reflect the occupation. The teal ink is
repeated in the variegated metallic thread zigzagged right into the
card. Loose thread ends dangle and add texture and visual
interest.

Cranford Creations

YOLANDA CRANFORD
FIBER ARTIST
◊
2824 SUMMIT RIDGE
GRAPEVINE, TEXAS 76051
◊
817/481-7845

Client   D.A. Case Associates, Inc.
              Minneapolis, Minnesota
Design Firm   Spangler Design Team
              St. Louis Park, Minnesota

Clean-edged images working in relationship with each other set an
appropriate tone for the card of manufacturers' representatives in the
high-tech industry.

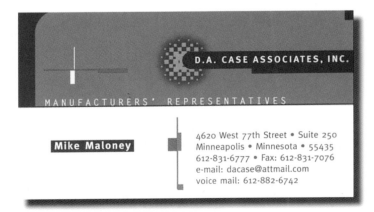

D.A. CASE ASSOCIATES, INC.

MANUFACTURERS' REPRESENTATIVES

Mike Maloney

4620 West 77th Street • Suite 250
Minneapolis • Minnesota • 55435
612-831-6777 • Fax: 612-831-7076
e-mail: dacase@attmail.com
voice mail: 612-882-6742

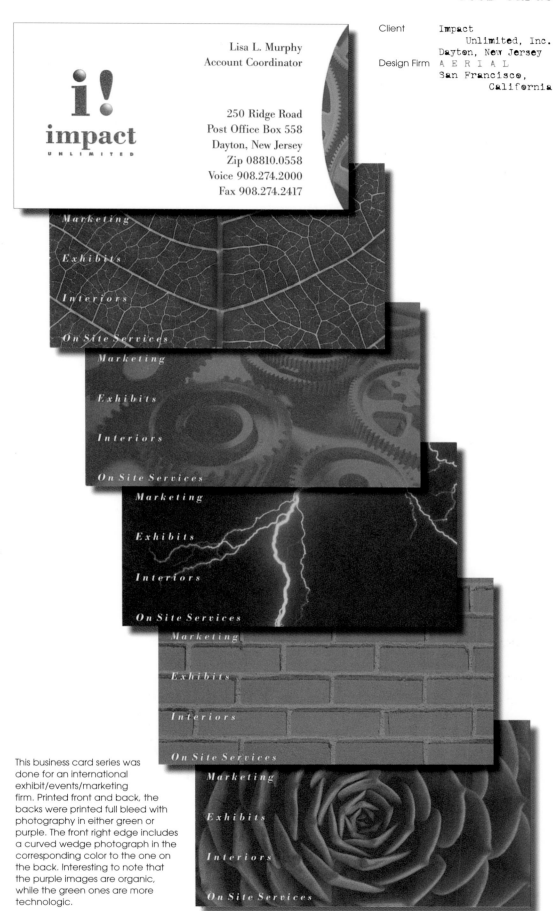

Lisa L. Murphy
Account Coordinator

250 Ridge Road
Post Office Box 558
Dayton, New Jersey
Zip 08810.0558
Voice 908.274.2000
Fax 908.274.2417

i!
impact
UNLIMITED

Client   Impact
             Unlimited, Inc.
             Dayton, New Jersey
Design Firm A E R I A L
             San Francisco,
             California

Marketing
Exhibits
Interiors
On Site Services

This business card series was done for an international exhibit/events/marketing firm. Printed front and back, the backs were printed full bleed with photography in either green or purple. The front right edge includes a curved wedge photograph in the corresponding color to the one on the back. Interesting to note that the purple images are organic, while the green ones are more technologic.

9

Mike Ousley

714 675 9600
fax/modem 675 9900
1544 Miramar Drive #3
Balboa CA 92661

DFacto

Client   DFacto
             Balboa, California
Design Firm DFacto
             Balboa, California

Smaller than typical size repeats the minimalist theme of this business card.

Lenore Henry-Whiteside

Executive Vice-President

1533 E. Avenue J-3

Lancaster, CA 93535

Phone 805 • 940 • 5953

Modem 805 • 945 • 2291

Client   Whiteside Design Studio
             Lancaster, California
Design Firm Steve Trapero Design
             Silver Spring, Maryland

An accordion-fold business card that deals strongly
with positive and negative space relates well to this
design studio's name.

Client   R.T. Jones, Capital Equities, Inc.
            St. Louis, Missouri
Design Firm CUBE Advertising & Design
            St. Louis, Missouri

R.T. Jones
Capital Equities, Inc.

Registered: Securities Broker
Dealer, Investment Advisors
Member NASD, S.I.P.C.

7911 Forsyth
Suite 560
Clayton, Missouri 63105
Telephone
314/727-2737

Arnold D. Tennant
Executive Vice President

Blind embossing on the front of this white business card adds a touch of elegance and subtly hints at the possession of money—very appropriate for the image of securities broker, dealer, investment advisors. Important information is printed in black on the inside.

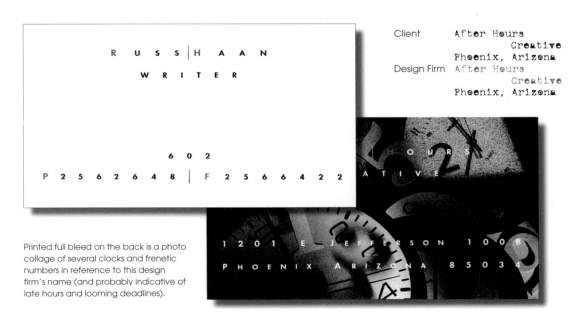

Client   After Hours
                      Creative
            Phoenix, Arizona
Design Firm After Hours
                      Creative
            Phoenix, Arizona

Printed full bleed on the back is a photo collage of several clocks and frenetic numbers in reference to this design firm's name (and probably indicative of late hours and looming deadlines).

CAPITOL HILL
SEVENTH-DAY
ADVENTIST CHURCH

John S. Nixon
Senior Pastor

914 Massachusetts Ave., NE
Washington, DC 20002
Phone 202.543.1344
Fax 202.543.0144
Email C-serve 74532.440

Client   Capitol Hill Seventh-Day Adventist Church
           Washington, D.C.
Design Firm Steve Trapero Design
           Silver Spring, Maryland

Business and calling cards are unified with line-textured stock, typography, color scheme, and consistent use of a Trinity-symbolic logo. The slightly narrow business card is strictly for the senior pastor's use, while the bifold calling card could be distributed by anyone. The back has a fill-in "My name is _____" and the inside offers church information of interest to a newcomer.

CAPITOL HILL
SEVENTH-DAY
ADVENTIST CHURCH

"Where all are Welcome

and Jesus Christ is Lord!"

914 Massachusetts Ave., NE
Washington, DC 20002
Phone 202.543.1344
Fax 202.543.0144

Services & Times
Church at Study
Saturdays 9:30 am

Sabbath Celebration
Saturday 11:00 am

Prayer Meeting
Wednesday 7:30 pm

Pastoral Staff
John S. Nixon
Senior Pastor

Ebenezer Pedapudi
Associate Pastor

PRINT MEDIA & DESIGN, INC.

SHERYL E. SCRUGGS-CROSS

P R E S I D E N T

701 E STREET, SE, SUITE 100
WASHINGTON, DC 20003
2 0 2 . 5 4 4 . 8 6 0 1
FAX 202.544.8603
E-MAIL pmdezin@mail.idt.net

Client   PMD-Print Media & Design, Inc.
            Washington, D.C.
Design Firm Steve Trapero Design
            Silver Spring, Maryland

An interesting logo utilizing the three initials of this design studio's name is an integral element of this card. Also distinctive is the use of justified type.

Client   Mighty Wrapps
             Minneapolis, Minnesota
Design Firm Spangler Design Team
             St. Louis Park, Minnesota

Lively graphics, colors, and typography make an eye-catching card for a restaurant that looks like fun.

Mighty Wrapps

Calhoun Sqaure
3001 Hennepin Ave. So.
Minneapolis, MN
55408

612-925-WRAP
Fax 824-1211

Nick Collins

Client   Franz & Company, Inc.
              Silver Spring, Maryland
Design Firm   Steve Trapero Design
              Silver Spring, Maryland

Lowercase sans serif letters in the logo are offset by the consistent use of serif capitals in the card's information area. Pink is printed full bleed on the back, echoing the single pink element, "f", on the front.

Client   Peter Shepley Photography, Inc.
              St. Louis, Missouri
Design Firm   CUBE Advertising & Design
              St. Louis, Missouri

The photographer's name is printed negatively in the area of the card resembling a photographer's negative strips. The word "photography" plays off the "P" in the owner's name.

id´i·om

Rick Bragdon
Partner

431 Jackson Street
San Francisco, CA
94111-1601

Tel 415.788.7248
Fax 415.982.2276

h
i

Client   Idiom
              San Francisco,
                   California
Design Firm   A E R I A L
              San Francisco,
                   California

The business card for a naming firm
is letterpressed and foil stamped
like a dictionary's index tab, and is
complete with dictionary definition
on the back.

id´i·om (ĭd´ē-əm) n. [Latin *idioma*, to make one's own.]
1. A significant verbal or visual expression with meaning
beyond its literal words or symbols. **2.** A singular statement
or style characteristic of a company or product. **3.** An elo-
quent artistic expression uniquely one's own.

Client   Culinary Arts & Entertainment
              Scottsdale, Arizona
Design Firm   After Hours Creative
              Phoenix, Arizona

A malfunctioning neon sign leaves burning the initials of the client's
name on this narrow business card.

culinary arts & entertainment
7610 e. mcdonald dr. suite h
scottsdale, az 85250
tel: 602 998 5810
tel: 800 211 5844
fax: 602 998 9064

Client   A E R I A L
              San Francisco,
                         California
Design Firm   A E R I A L
              San Francisco,
                         California

This amazing set of business cards is part
of a series which is added to each year.
Each card back has usual business card
information.

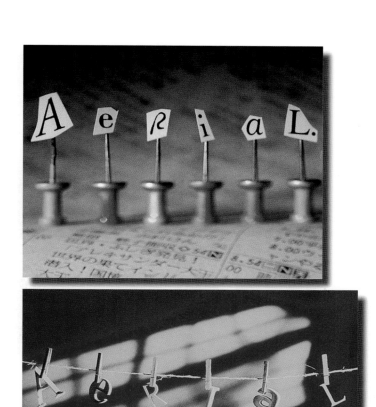

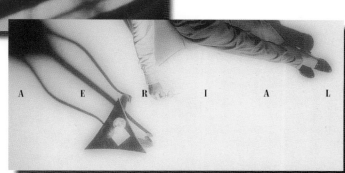

ART KANE STUDIO, INC.

568 BROADWAY · NY, NY 10012 · TEL. 212 925 7334

Client   Art Kane
              New York, New York
Design Firm   Designation, Inc.
              New York, New York

Interesting Transformer®-type figure is created out of photographer's equipment for a photography studio—**SuperPhotographer**, right?

Client   Lambert Design
              Dallas, Texas
Design Firm   Lambert
                   Design
              Dallas, Texas

Unusually shaped business cards are wide ovals turned at approximately 22° and printed. One side is printed full bleed with the firm's logo in three colors. The opposite side is strictly typographic, but also is printed in three colors.

LAMBERT DESIGN

Call 214.987.3070

Fax 987.0170

Or just come by 7007 Twin Hills Ave.

Suite No. 213

Dallas, Texas 75231

CHRISTIE LAMBERT RASMUSSEN

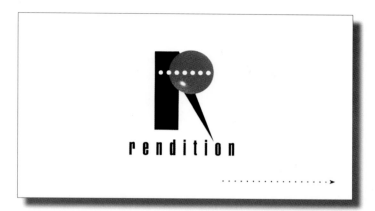

Client   Rendition
             Mountain View,
                   California
Design Firm Mortensen
                      Design
             Mountain View,
                   California

Graphic elements are grouped to create the Gestalt of an "R" for this business that creates software allowing high speed 3-D graphic rendering for the PC. The orb is embossed on one side; necessarily debossed on the other. Arrow and dot elements are repeated on both sides of the business card urging the viewer to turn it over.

Client   Vanderschuit Photography
             San Diego, California
Design Firm Mires Design, Inc.
             San Diego, California

A solution found in typography creates a very clean card and makes the photographer's name memorable. Notice that this would not have been successful if the card had been used horizontally.

V
Joan Hix VanderSchuit
A
VanderSchuit
N
Studio Inc.
D
751 Turquoise
E
San Diego
R
California
S
92109-1034
C
Telephone
H
619-539-7337
U
Facsimile
I
619-539-2081
T

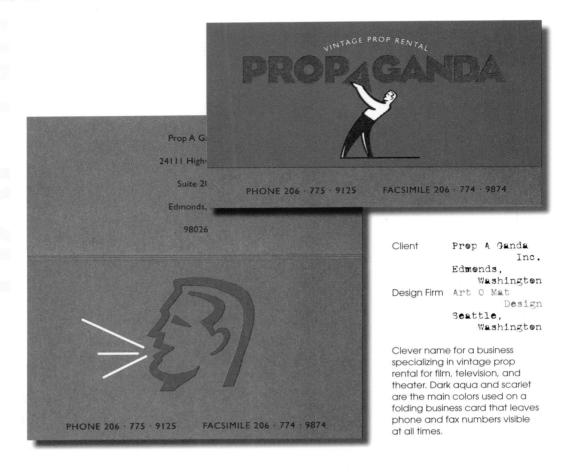

VINTAGE PROP RENTAL

PROP A GANDA

Prop A G...

24111 High...

Suite 2(

Edmonds,

98026

PHONE 206 · 775 · 9125   FACSIMILE 206 · 774 · 9874

PHONE 206 · 775 · 9125   FACSIMILE 206 · 774 · 9874

Client   Prop A Ganda
                        Inc.
              Edmonds,
                   Washington
Design Firm   Art O Mat
                        Design
              Seattle,
                   Washington

Clever name for a business
specializing in vintage prop
rental for film, television, and
theater. Dark aqua and scarlet
are the main colors used on a
folding business card that leaves
phone and fax numbers visible
at all times.

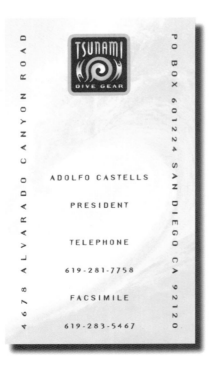

TSUNAMI
DIVE GEAR

4678 ALVARADO CANYON ROAD

ADOLFO CASTELLS

PRESIDENT

TELEPHONE

619-281-7758

FACSIMILE

619-283-5467

P O BOX 601224 SAN DIEGO CA 92120

Client   Tsunami Dive Gear
              San Diego, California
Design Firm   Mires Design, Inc.
              San Diego, California

A huge wave is printed monochromatically, full bleed, as an
appropriate background on this business card for a dive gear
company. Logo and type colors are not-so-typical shades of
purple and golden yellow.

2224 EAST ADAMS STREET
TUCSON, AZ 85719 USA
PH 520.327.7850
FX 520.321.1858
dbf@primenet.com

THE FRESHWATER GROUP

DIANA BARNES FRESHWATER
PRINCIPAL

Client   The Freshwater Group
              Tucson, Arizona
Design Firm   Boelts Bros., Associates
              Tucson, Arizona

Purple and black are paired on this colorful, but easy-to-read card.
Indicative of rain (freshwater) clouds, clouds in the logo are printed purple
coordinating with the black background with purple lines. The purple line
is repeated through the name of the company's letters—looks nice.

Client   AquaPenn Spring Water Co.
              Milesburg, Pennsylvania
Design Firm   Sommese Design
              State College, Pennsylvania

A die-cut, embossed, folded, vertical business card is very
distinctive. The color aqua is a visual play on the name of the
company. The closed cover is simple, but striking: clean white with
the company name printed in aqua. At the top, in aqua, the logo
breaks the edge of the card almost as a pop-up. Inside card is
printed full bleed aqua with type reversed in white.

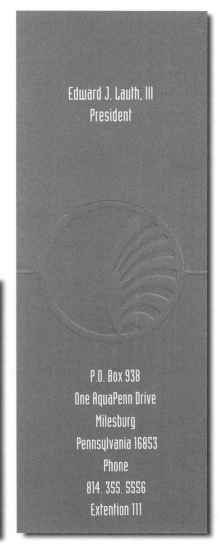

Edward J. Lauth, III
President

P.O. Box 938
One AquaPenn Drive
Milesburg
Pennsylvania 16853
Phone
814. 355. 5556
Extention 111

AquaPenn spring water company

Client   Junglee Corporation
                Sunnyvale, California
Design Firm Mortensen Design
                Mountain View, California

"Junglee is the first company to develop and market virtual database (VDB) technology that enables enterprise and content publishers to automatically aggregate vital data from the Internet, corporate intranets, and legacy data sources and deliver this data to core business applications."

Bright colors, clean lines and an effective juxtaposition of letters "J" and "e".

Client   Mires Design, Inc.
                San Diego, California
Design Firm Mires Design, Inc.
                San Diego, California

Extra heavy stock gives this card a stability that translates to the identity of the design firm. Rounded corners and justified type are also unique touches.

MIRES DESIGN INC

2345 KETTNER BLVD SAN DIEGO CA 92101

PHONE: 619 234 6631 FAX: 619 234 1807

E MAIL: MIRES@MIRESDESIGN.COM

SCOTT MIRES

LANNY SOMMESE
DESIGN & ILLUSTRATION
481 GLENN ROAD
STATE COLLEGE
PENNSYLVANIA, 16803
814 238 7484

LANNY SOMMESE
DESIGN & ILLUSTRATION
481 GLENN ROAD
STATE COLLEGE
PENNSYLVANIA, 16803
814 238 7484

LANNY SOMMESE
PROFESSOR AND HEAD
GRAPHIC DESIGN
PENN STATE UNIVERSITY
110 PATTERSON BUILDING
UNIVERSITY PARK
PENNSYLVANIA, 16802
814 865 1203

LANNY SOMMESE
CORRESPONDENT, NOVUM
GEBRAUCHSGRAPHIK
110 PATTERSON BUILDING
UNIVERSITY PARK
PENNSYLVANIA, 16802
814 865 1203

LANNY SOMMESE
CORRESPONDENT, NOVUM
GEBRAUCHSGRAPHIK
110 PATTERSON BUILDING
UNIVERSITY PARK
PENNSYLVANIA, 16802
814 865 1203

LANNY SOMMESE
PROFESSOR AND HEAD
GRAPHIC DESIGN
PENN STATE UNIVERSITY
110 PATTERSON BUILDING
UNIVERSITY PARK
PENNSYLVANIA, 16802
814 865 1203

LANNY SOMMESE
CORRESPONDENT, NOVUM
GEBRAUCHSGRAPHIK
110 PATTERSON BUILDING
UNIVERSITY PARK
PENNSYLVANIA, 16802
814 865 1203

LANNY SOMMESE
PROFESSOR AND HEAD
GRAPHIC DESIGN
PENN STATE UNIVERSITY
110 PATTERSON BUILDING
UNIVERSITY PARK
PENNSYLVANIA, 16802
814 865 1203

Client   Lanny Sommese
              State College, Pennsylvania
Design Firm   Sommese Design
              State College, Pennsylvania

Incorporating three job descriptions into one card is a problem solved in the above execution. Three types of cards (vertical fold, horizontal fold, and single cards) were printed with three similar but different icons. In the initial L's negative space one finds a figure comprised of at least one hand and foot representing each respective occupation. For design and illustration, a t-square is added. A correspondent needs two feet. A professor and head of graphic design can always use an extra hand.

4530 West Pine
Suite 100
St. Louis, MO
63108

MARY McELWAIN

314 361 3701

Client   McElwain Fine Arts
              St. Louis, Missouri
Design Firm   Bartels & Company, Inc.
              St. Louis, Missouri

Printed in black and white except for the lone blue, red, and
yellow letters, this vertical business card still demands attention.
Justified type reversed out of a black block is repeated in the
treatment of the cardholder's name.

530 Maryville Centre
Suite LL10
Saint Louis, Missouri 63141-5821
(314) 434-3434 • Fax 434-1727

Client   Fair Saint Louis
              St. Louis, Missouri
Design Firm   Bartels & Company, Inc.
              St. Louis, Missouri

Complementary color scheme of blue and orange was chosen
for a business card for an annual Fourth of July festival. Even if
you couldn't read, Gateway Arch and fleur de lis hint strongly at
the St. Louis location.

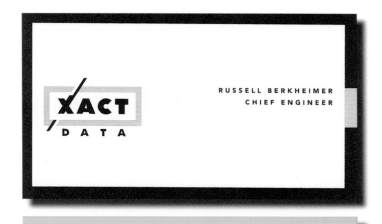

RUSSELL BERKHEIMER
CHIEF ENGINEER

DIRECT: 206 382 6618
MAIN: 206 654 5300
FAX: 206 382 6615
INTERNET:
russb@xactdata.com

XACTDATA CORPORATION
ONE UNION SQUARE
600 UNIVERSITY STREET
SUITE 911
SEATTLE WA 98101

Client   XactData Corporation
                Seattle, Washington
Design Firm   Hornall Anderson Design Works, Inc.
                Seattle, Washington

All caps/small caps along with lined stock set a tone of preciseness for this distributive system back-up company. Black and golden yellow colors with full bleed printing lend the card its individuality.

Client   Teri Bianchi DDS
                Westlake Village, California
Design Firm   Talbot Design
                Westlake Village, California

Script typeface in a calm gray/green adds softness to this card's layout. In order to be able to identify at a glance the business represented, an image that looks very much like a molar x-ray was added.

Teri Bianchi DDS
Family Dentistry

Denise Poprocki
Office Manager

805 230 2293

1240 South Westlake Boulevard
Suite 127
Westlake Village CA
91361

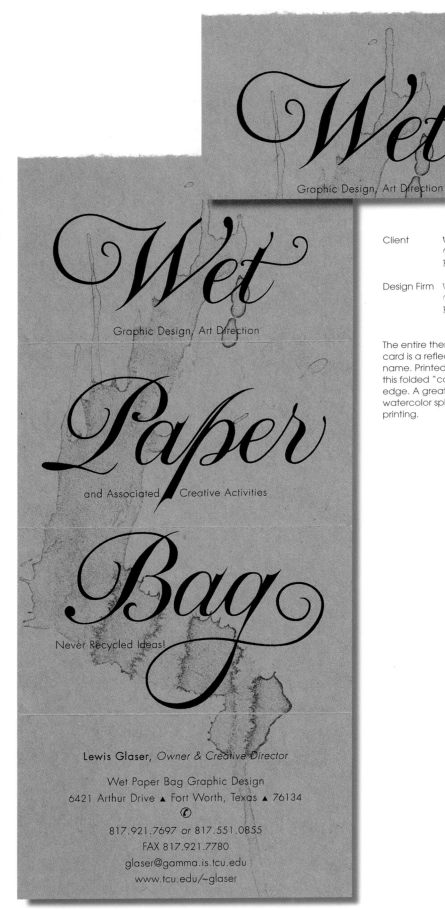

Wet

Graphic Design, Art Direction

Wet

Graphic Design, Art Direction

Paper

and Associated Creative Activities

Bag

Never Recycled Ideas!

Lewis Glaser, *Owner & Creative Director*

Wet Paper Bag Graphic Design
6421 Arthur Drive ▲ Fort Worth, Texas ▲ 76134
ⓒ
817.921.7697 or 817.551.0855
FAX 817.921.7780
glaser@gamma.is.tcu.edu
www.tcu.edu/~glaser

Client	Wet Paper Bag Graphic Design Fort Worth, Texas
Design Firm	Wet Paper Bag Graphic Design Fort Worth, Texas

The entire theme of this business card is a reflection of the firm's name. Printed on brown paper, this folded "card" has a torn top edge. A great final touch is watercolor splashed over the printing.

#include

Steve Payne

\# Analytical Services
\# Application Development
\# Technical Writing
\# Outsource for Application Support

243 Princeton Street, Jefferson, MA 01522 # 508-829-5597

Client   #include
             Jefferson, Massachusetts
Design Firm Janet Payne Graphic Designer
             Hopewell, New Jersey

To reduce some of the rigidness in a computer consultant's image, a faint "# "sign is created in a watercolor wash as a background for the necessary information on this card.

Client   John Trippiedi
             Los Angeles, California
Design Firm J. Robert Faulkner
             Venice, California

Blue handprints make a memorable image in a relaxing color for a client whose business is massage. Minimal type info includes service offered, name, and pager number.

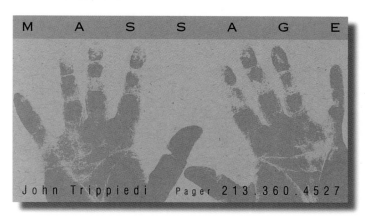

A-OK

Client   Black Cat Images Inc.
              Evansville, Indiana
Design Firm   Gregory R. Farmer Design
              Evansville, Indiana

This striking business card is thermoengraved in black and red on both sides. Heavy stock seems to be double thickness of regular weight cards. The slashing image in the logo is repeated in one of the card's fonts.

Client   Chiow Communication
              St. Louis, Missouri
Design Firm   CUBE Advertising & Design
              St. Louis, Missouri

Yellow, black, and white symmetrical geometric shapes comprise this larger-than-usual business card. The thoughtful, if somewhat symbolic, name logo utilizes a die cut to form the iconic eye for the letter "I" in the name, "Chiow".

STEVE TRAPERO

ART DIRECTOR / DESIGNER

STEVE TRAPERO DESIGN

3309-G HAMPTON POINT DRIVE

SILVER SPRING, MD 20904

301.847.9462

Client   Steve Trapero Design
                    Silver Spring, Maryland

Design Firm Steve Trapero Design
                    Silver Spring, Maryland

This wide, short card utilizes a type of vellum for its stock. Nearly transparent and lighter weight than most cards, it is surprisingly sturdy.

D·A·Y P·U·N·C·H

A division of Universal Manufacturing

Client   Day Punch
                    Kansas City,
                           Missouri

Design Firm Russell Leong
                           Design
                    Palo Alto,
                         California

A great example of incorporating this calendar punching manufacturer's work right into the business card, the front is punched for each day of the week leaving a dot of yellow showing through each hole. Open the card for information.

Tony Wightman
President

Daypunch, Inc.
Universal Manufacturing Co.
5450 Deramus, Kansas City, MO 64120
1-800-821-2724 • 1-816-231-2771 • Fax 816-483-6842

Client   Lipham & Associates
             Madison, Wisconsin
Design Firm Z•D Studios, Inc.
             Madison, Wisconsin

Since woodcuts were one of the first forms of advertising art,
woodcut images in purple echo this marketing/advertising
company's name. Full-bleed printing allows text to be either
reversed out of a purple background or printed in gold.

Client   Tom Rooney
             Portland, Oregon
Design Firm Harry 3
             Muse Design
             Santa Fe, New Mexico

Special photographic effects of the space-alien description adorn
this photographer's card. Atypical design includes vertical format
on one side and horizontal on the flip.

Client   Yvett & Greg Chevalier
              West Linn, Oregon
Design Firm   Talbot Design
              Westlake Village, California

A bright green, computer-generated wave comes out of the black
background to hover behind and above a gradient purple tagline—very
unusual card for a business that deals with sales/distribution.

Client   Harry MacDonald Forehand III
              Futureboy Industries
              Santa Fe, New Mexico
Design Firm   Harry 3
              Muse Design
              Santa Fe, New Mexico

With eerie purples, a spacecraft-like icon, and absolutely no information
except a phone number in futuristic form this card really entices a call.

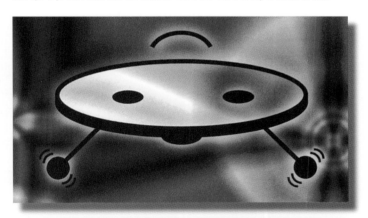

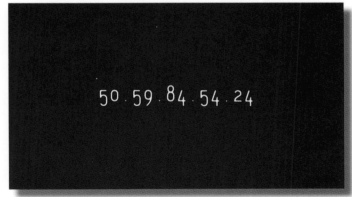

Client   ACS Communications
              Scotts Valley, California
Design Firm   Kevin Akers
              San Rafael, California

Concentric circles representing sound and hearing make a symbolic background for a headset manufacturer. Darker cyan has type reversed in white or printed yellow.

Client   Tharp Did It
              Los Gatos,
                    California
Design Firm   Tharp Did It
              Los Gatos,
                    California

Different images adorn different cards for this design firm. The backs of business cards are hand stamped with various messages, but one phrase is always kept in mind, "Tharp Did It."

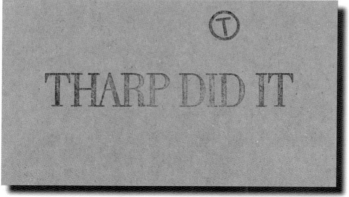

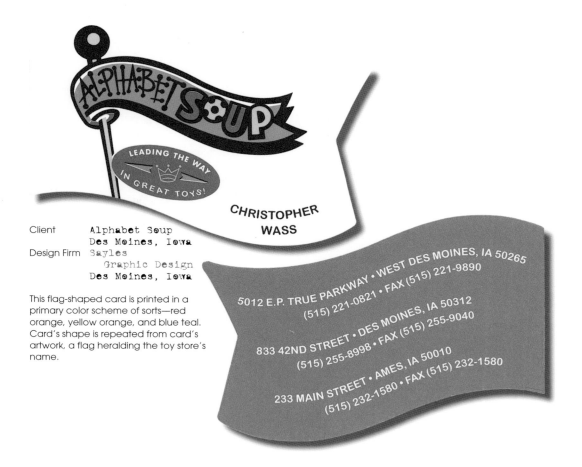

LEADING THE WAY
IN GREAT TOYS!

CHRISTOPHER
WASS

Client Alphabet Soup
Des Moines, Iowa
Design Firm Sayles
Graphic Design
Des Moines, Iowa

This flag-shaped card is printed in a primary color scheme of sorts—red orange, yellow orange, and blue teal. Card's shape is repeated from card's artwork, a flag heralding the toy store's name.

5012 E.P. TRUE PARKWAY • WEST DES MOINES, IA 50265
(515) 221-0821 • FAX (515) 221-9890

833 42ND STREET • DES MOINES, IA 50312
(515) 255-8998 • FAX (515) 255-9040

233 MAIN STREET • AMES, IA 50010
(515) 232-1580 • FAX (515) 232-1580

Client Graphic Marketing Organization, Inc.
Lancaster, Pennsylvania
Design Firm Dean Design/Marketing Group
Lancaster, Pennsylvania

This printing broker's card is printed with the basics of four-color printing: cyan, yellow, magenta, and black. Basic geometric shapes of triangle, square, and circle are used as design elements and quite effectively as letters in the company name.

GMO

275 Hess Boulevard
Lancaster, PA 17601
P 717-581-5000
F 717-581-8116

William Holliday
President

GR▲PHIC
MARKETI■G
ORGANIZATI●N,
INC.

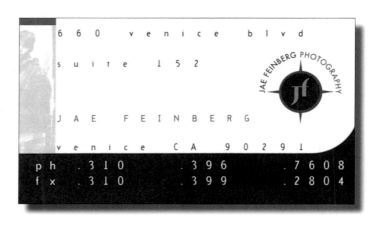

Client   Jae Feinberg
              Venice, California
Design Firm   Talbot Design
              Westlake Village, California

Loosely-kerned typography and lots of white space create an air of spaciousness on a limited surface area. Repeated curves and a sample of the photographer's work make sure this card is different from most.

Client   Mac Forehand/LANL
              Los Alamos,
                     New Mexico
Design Firm   Harry 3
              Muse Design
              Santa Fe,
                     New Mexico

Technical/mechanical elements are an appropriate choice for the background texture of a card for the holder of a Ph.D. in nuclear engineering. Artwork is printed full bleed on the back of the business card. On the front, it's printed negatively and bleeds off three sides. Bright green type is easily read on a dark blue surface.

Dick Bitzer
founder,
chairman of
the board

BAYSHORE PRESS

103 Whispering Pines Dr.

Scotts Valley, Calif. 95066

Facsimile 408.439.8888

Telephone 408.439.8100

1.800.400.3266

Printed on a 100% post-consumer recycled non-deinked paper.

Client   Bayshore Press
                Scotts Valley,
                        California
Design Firm Tharp Did It
                Los Gatos, California

Paper turning into flying birds is full of symbolism—freedom, letting your mind take flight, no limits...Slightly debossed paper image adds texture to a speckled card stock.

Client   Mad City Cafe
                Madison, Wisconsin
Design Firm Z•D Studios, Inc.
                Madison, Wisconsin

Neutrals blue, green, and red work well together. Loose application of color and a handwritten-style font indicate a fun and relaxed restaurant.

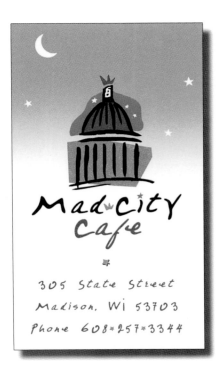

Mad City
Cafe

305 State Street
Madison, WI 53703
Phone 608•257•3344

SANDRA FAIRBANK DESIGN
◆
Interiors

180 Franklin Street
Cambridge MA 02139

Tel 617.497.0693
Fax 617.497.6988

email:
FairDesign@aol.com

Client	Sandra Fairbank Design Cambridge, Massachusetts
Design Firm	Fyfe Design Cambridge, Massachusetts

Heavy vellum printed with a pale ticking stripe, reminiscent of both fabric and wallpaper, is a good choice for the base of an interior designer's card. Pale green sans serif type complements the elegant simplicity of this design perfectly.

BEACH HOUSE
INN & CONFERENCE CENTER

4100 NORTH CABRILLO HIGHWAY
HALF MOON BAY, CALIFORNIA 94019

TEL 415.712.0220
FAX 415.712.0693
800.315.9366

VIEW@BEACH-HOUSE.COM

ocean lofts

DAVID C. SMITH
CHIEF OPERATING OFFICER

Client	Beach House Inn & Conference Center Half Moon Bay, California
Design Firm	AERIAL San Francisco, California

Rippled sand printed full bleed supports the information on one side of this delicately die cut business card. Nice blue and tan colors are great beach tones. The half moon window is so evocative of shore life, surely the ocean can be seen on the other side!

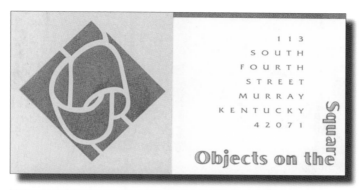

Client   Objects on the Square
              Murray, Kentucky
Design Firm   Gregory R. Farmer Design
              Evansville, Indiana

Even though only one bronze-colored ink is used in the printing of this card the impression of more colors is left because of the use of screens, gradients, and a card stock that is different colors on either side.

Client   Cosmopolitan Grill
              San Francisco, California
Design Firm   Tharp Did It
              Los Gatos, California

Unusual wedge-shaped business card repeats the shape in the restaurant name's type. The restaurant's name is gold foil stamped with gray and metallic gray blue inks completing the color scheme. On the back of the card, reversed out of full bleed metallic gray blue, are initial caps in two very different, but successfully coordinated styles: the "C" is a very structured sans serif letter, while the "G" is much freer in a scribbled manner.

Client   Just One Recordings
              Atlanta, Georgia
Design Firm   After Hours Creative
              Phoenix, Arizona

Gold-colored and metallic blue inks are the complementary colors
chosen for this company. The logo is nicely done with the number "1"
formed in the negative space of the "U" in "Just". Rounded corners and
outline type look quite futuristic in this instance.

Client   EDCO Builders
              Eagle Rock, California
Design Firm   Steve Trapero Design
              Silver Spring, Maryland

Dark blue ink matches fibered card stock perfectly, but the nicest part of
this design for a general contractor is the image of screened nails in the
background.

SCOTT BATDORFF
PRINT DEPARTMENT MANAGER

CALYPSO IMAGING, INC.
2000 MARTIN AVENUE
SANTA CLARA, CALIFORNIA
ZIP 95050.2700

TEL 408.727.2318
TOLL FREE 800.794.2755
FAX 408.727.1705

Client   Calypso Imaging, Inc.
             Santa Clara, California
Design Firm A E R I A L
             San Francisco, California

A variety of colors with the same tonal values are a good mix without being too loud. Also notice the mix of fonts in the company name. Business card front and back have different directional orientation; the back being printed monochromatically with a full bleed.

IMAGES/EVERYTHING

Client   Sande Thomas
             Evansville, Indiana
Design Firm Gregory R. Farmer Design
             Evansville, Indiana

Humorous bubble wrap texture is printed with a three-sided bleed on the back of this heavy vellum business card. The artist's name, services, and address are in black on the front. A reptilian watermark hides in the white space at the bottom of the card.

SANDE THOMAS
ARTIST • DESIGNER

UNIQUE MULTIMEDIA OBJECTS, DESIGNS, & FINISHES FOR COMMERCIAL AND RESIDENTIAL ENVIRONMENTS.

616 WEST MT. PLEASANT ROAD
EVANSVILLE, INDIANA 47711
812.
867.5280

You spoke to:

_____

Name

BLUE Clothing in Dornbirn:

Marktplatz (Hirschenhaus), A 6850 Dornbirn, Austria

Please call us at: 05572 36 840-0

When abroad, dial: 43 5572 36 840-0

YES! We do speak German.

Client   Blue
          Austria
Design Firm Sagmeister
                    Inc.
          New York,
               New York

The typical color answer for this card would have been taken from the business name, but instead, just the opposite was chosen. Blocks of orange and black leave a memorable image. The name of this fashion retailer is found again in the facial features of figures reversed out of black (different cards have different variations). Flip side of the card offers location information.

Client   Country Fair Farms
          Westminster, Maryland
Design Firm Dean Design/Marketing Group
          Lancaster, Pennsylvania

Hens and eggs are pretty general icons for an egg producer, but the clear colors of this business card—yellow, red, blue, green—combine to form an aura of warmth and wholesomeness.

695 BACHMANS VALLEY ROAD
WESTMINSTER, MD 21157
410•876•1825

Printed on recycled paper.

Client   Lee Masters
               San Francisco, California
Design Firm   Kevin Akers
               San Rafael, California

Maroon, pink, and orange are a unique color scheme for an interesting image. An armadillo, created in paper-cutout style, adorns this personal calling card.

Client   Azalea
               Birmingham, Alabama
Design Firm   Walter McCord Graphic Design
               Louisville, Kentucky

Very loose pen-and-ink drawing of a woman holding a fish and bottle of wine is plainly for a restaurant's business card. Adding more visual interest are the loose color applications "behind" the food elements. Orange felt tip pen shadows the fish. Green watercolor highlights the wine.

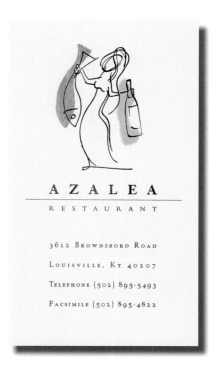

AZALEA
RESTAURANT

3612 BROWNSBORO ROAD

LOUISVILLE, KY 40207

TELEPHONE (502) 895-5493

FACSIMILE (502) 895-4822

VICIOUS CYCLE
MOUNTAIN BIKES

JOHN LARSON

204 SOUTH THIRD ST
RICHMOND, KY 40475
TEL: (606) 626-8715
FAX: (606) 626-1236

Client   Vicious Cycle
              Richmond, Kentucky
Design Firm   Walter McCord & Mary Cawein
                              Graphic Design
              Louisville, Kentucky

Simply executed but well devised, an angry dog chasing his own
tail is a perfect image for "Vicious Cycle". (You've got to love that
name when you realize the company sells mountain bikes.)

Client   Quantum
              Madison, Wisconsin
Design Firm   Z•D Studios, Inc.
              Madison, Wisconsin

Repetition of triangles is found in this business card's design. The logo has
a triangle invading a circle which forms a "Q", the initial of the business.
The same triangle forms an "A" in the company name, and a series of
triangles is used as design elements along the edge of the card.

QUANTUM
COMMERCIAL

Cathy A. Weisensel
Office Manager

8401 GREENWAY BLVD
MIDDLETON, WI 53562
PHONE [608]836.6646
FAX   [608]836.6656

Client   Cisneros Design
              Santa Fe, New Mexico
Design Firm   Harry 3
              Cisneros Design
              Santa Fe, New Mexico

Unusually small (1-3/4" x 1-3/4") cards are beautifully printed in four-color process, but are more intriguing because of the missing information. Only first names are listed—no address or phone.

Client   Homemakers Schools, Inc.
              Madison, Wisconsin
Design Firm   Z•D Studios, Inc.
              Madison, Wisconsin

An aqua and pink colored-pencil illustration of a cut cake is the icon for this cooking school for women. It's positioned on (and off) a black slab that looks much like scratchboard with a little pink showing through from the other side.

Client   Lamar Snowboards
              San Diego, California
Design Firm   Talbot Design
              Westlake Village, California

Green and black ink used with coarse screens is reminiscent of comic
books and ACTION characters. Nice die cut on the bottom edge of the
card mimics the edge of a snowboard, the client's product.

Client   The Dandy Candy Man
              Los Gatos, California
Design Firm   Tharp Did It
              Los Gatos, California

A very professional-looking card for a novelty candy company
pictures a well-dressed, but questionable, character offering
candy. He looks much like the stranger of "don't take candy
from strangers" fame. He's humorously suited for his iconic role;
The Dandy Candy Man is a purveyor of condommints.

KELLY O'CONNOR
HEAD CANDY MAN

THE DANDY CANDY MAN

Purveyor of Condommints

●

POST OFFICE BOX 2151

LOS GATOS, CA 95031

P H O N E · 408.378.5600

TELEFAX · 408.354.1450

Client   The Electric
                   Chair
           Madison,
                  Wisconsin
Design Firm   Z•D Studios, Inc.
          Madison,
                 Wisconsin

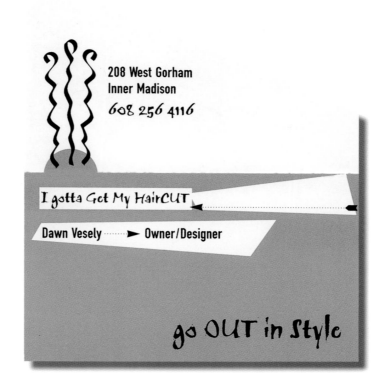

Funny name for a hair salon is the beginning of a folded business card that surely won't be forgotten. Unique die cut on the cover's bottom edge, grunge typeface in association with a more traditional sans serif, and unusually-angled shapes reflecting the front cover all combine to create a very distinct identity.

FREDA SCOTT

FREDA SCOTT, INC.
1015-B BATTERY ST.
SAN FRANCISCO, CA
94111
☎ 415.398.9121
FAX 415.398.6136

ARTISTS REPRESENTATIVE

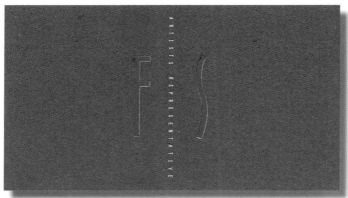

ARTISTS REPRESENTATIVE

Client   Freda Scott
             San Francisco,
                California
Design Firm Russell Leong
                Design
             Palo Alto,
                California

Double-sided card stock
contains flecks of color much like
handmade papers. Muted
purple and green inks coordinate beautifully with colored
flecks. On the flip side, a solid
green with flecks, the
cardholder's initials are copper
foil stamped.

Client   Bird Design
             Cambridge, Massachusetts
Design Firm Fyfe Design
             (formerly Bird Design)
             Cambridge, Massachusetts

An embossed bird's egg, printed and varnished, makes a delicate
but distinctive statement on this design firm's business card.

BIRD DESIGN

875 MAIN STREET
CAMBRIDGE, MA 02139
FAX 617-876-9124
617-491-7491

JENNIFER MCPHILIMY

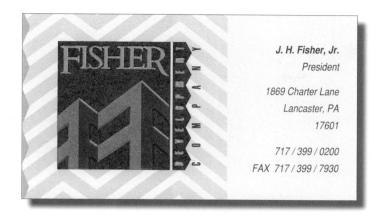

Client   Fisher Development Company
             Lancaster, Pennsylvania
Design Firm Dean Design/Marketing Group, Inc.
             Lancaster, Pennsylvania

Gold foil stamping and embossing add extra visual interest to a well-designed card. Brick red and green inks, in accordance with embossed upward arrows that could very well be trees, suggest a harmonious balance between nature and urban development. A sense of environmental well being would be important for this developer of malls and corporate buildings.

Client   University Village
             Seattle, Washington
Design Firm Hornall Anderson Design Works, Inc.
             Seattle, Washington

Everything about this card works together to leave an impression of community—as opposed to megapolis. Calming green color, a loosely drawn tree logo, even the name incorporating the word "village" make this retail shopping center seem a place that feels comfortable, not threatening.

Client   City of Palo Alto Recreation
                 Palo Alto, California
Design Firm   Russell Leong Design
                 Palo Alto, California

Certainly straying from conventional sizes and shapes, these oversized business cards are 3″ round and 3-1/2″ x 4″ rectangle. The printing is black on white in reference to the event touted, Black & White Ball.

Client   Creatures of Habit
             Paducah, Kentucky
Design Firm Gregory R. Farmer Design
             Evansville, Indiana

JACK CODY &
NATALYA HADEN
OWNERS

creatures

■ COSTUME RENTAL

■ ■ ANTIQUES

■ VINTAGE CLOTHING

of habit

406 BROADWAY

PADUCAH, KY 42001

502.442.2923

This business card for an antiques and collectibles store incorporates many kinds of images throughout its three sides—drawings,
photographs, negative photos. The actual stock is gold, but full
bleed printing on one side leaves the impression of two colors of
paper.

toto kiki usa, inc.

sam coker
regional sales manager

415 west taft avenue unit a
orange, california 92665
telephone +1 714 282 8686
facsimile +1 714 282 1541

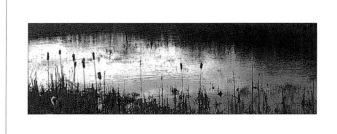

TOTO

TOTO

TOTO

Client	Toto
	Atlanta,
	Georgia
Design Firm	Sagmeister
	Inc.
	New York,
	New York

TOTO

TOTO

TOTO

For a company that deals with water related products, the backs of this series of business cards each has a different photograph of some type of water.

TOTO

Client   Sarasota Outlet Center
              University Park, Florida
Design Firm   Dean Design/Marketing Group
              Lancaster, Pennsylvania

Bright colors can sometimes compete for attention but this choice of pink and orange complement each other while being balanced by the blue. Notice the grass element from the logo enlarged and repeated in the bottom right corner.

Client   Iowa State Fair
              Des Moines, Iowa
Design Firm   Sayles Graphic Design
              Des Moines, Iowa

The Iowa State Fair must be a really fun time if its business card is any indication. Printed only in two colors, screens and interspersing the white background as a color makes it seem like there are more. Especially clever is that nearly every letter in the event name is an image from a fair food or festivity.

INK-WELL

ONE FERN ROAD
KENTFIELD, CA 94904
PHONE 415/925-9295
FAX 415/925-9296

MARCIA SKINNER

Client   Ink-Well
              Kentfield, California
Design Firm   Kevin Akers
              San Rafael, California

Slightly narrow business card has several "extras". Ink well and dropper are embossed and printed on a textured stock. Different color ink splashes are very eye-catching for this print broker's information.

Client   Kay Forehand
              Los Alamos,
              New Mexico
Design Firm   Harry 3
              Muse Design
              Santa Fe,
              New Mexico

The lively colors and comical images on this dental hygienist's business card have got to take some of the pain out of going to the dentist. Chattering teeth on the front and an Elvis-like cartoon on the back both have beautiful smiles—obviously from regular checkups.

Client   801 Steak and
                  Chop House
              Des Moines,
                      Iowa
Design Firm   Sayles Graphic
                      Design
              Des Moines,
                      Iowa

Illustrated card front in maroon, dark green, and black sets a tone with bold graphics and unrefined edges. There are two business card backs. One is solely informational with addresses and numbers of two additional eateries reversed out of full bleed green. The other is a monochromatic green screened photo of three cows—**probably** not your dinner.

Client   Phil Rudy Photography
              Fresno, California
Design Firm   Shields Design
              Fresno, California

Smooth Swiss dotted stock is the base for a business card that shows a vintage camera for this photographer's identity. Understatement works well in ink colors.

Phil Rudy

764 P Street • Suite D • Fresno, CA 93721 • 209-441-1887

Frances Lee Jasper
Oriental Rugs

Quad 7
1330 Bardstown Road
Louisville
Kentucky 40204
502 459-1044

Client   Jasper Oriental Rugs
              Louisville, Kentucky
Design Firm   Walter McCord Graphic Design
              Louisville, Kentucky

Larger than typical card offers a charming top-bleed
photo of a small child beating an oriental rug.

MARRONE BROS., INC.
GENERAL CONTRACTORS
POST OFFICE BOX FC
LOS GATOS, CA 95031
500 E. McGLINCEY LANE
CAMPBELL, CA 95008
GREG MARRONE
408.371.4003

LICENSE 536429

Client   Marrone
              Bros., Inc.
              Los Gatos,
              California
Design Firm   Tharp Did It
              Los Gatos,
              California

Developing noncliche imagery for
a general contractor might test
creative skills, but this solution is
great. On the front is a photograph
of a nail hammered into the card.
Turn the card over to find the nail
point coming out the other side.
Also interesting is a "quality" stamp
in the upper right corner of the
card front.

Bill Emberley Productions · 1479 Folsom St. · San Francisco, CA · 94103 · 415.252.9808 · Fx 415.252.9806

1479 Folsom St. · San Francisco, CA · 94103 · 415.252.9808 · Fx 415.252.9806

Bill Emberley Productions

Client   Bill Emberley Productions
              San Francisco, California
Design Firm   Kevin Akers
              San Rafael, California

Two kinds of business cards for this video producer offer the chance to court two types of clients: traditional, and the more avant garde. White card is a good quality, textured stock, but the black one is actually printed on acetate in two colors.

Client   STINKWEEDS
              Kimber Lanning
              Tempe, Arizona
Design Firm   Harry 3
              Muse Design
              Santa Fe,
              New Mexico

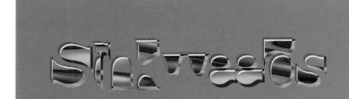

new · used · indies · imports · cds · vinyl · shirts · zines
1250 east apache #109 · tempe, az 85281
phone 602.968.9490 · fax 602.968.2131

STINKWEEDS

Surreal negative space elements create the name of the record store on the front. A full bleed bright green background works successfully with the rainbow of other colors chosen for the front. On the back is full bleed black with the business name in blurry gray.

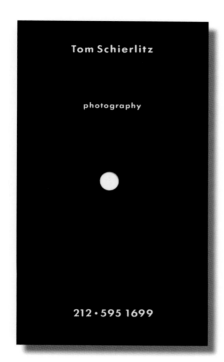

Tom Schierlitz

photography

212 • 595 1699

Client   Tom Schierlitz
                  New York, New York
Design Firm   Sagmeister Inc.
                  New York, New York

A card that is so clean in design may look simple, but is often the most difficult to execute. Name, service, and phone reverse out of black that bleeds off four sides, while a perfectly-centered, die cut circle leaves the impression of a camera lens.

Client   SandCastle
                  Tumon, Guam
Design Firm   Bartels &
                  Company, Inc.
                  St. Louis,
                  Missouri

Located on Guam, this dinner theater has a multi-cultural clientele. Lift card cover for a native language.

Client   Harry MacDonald Forehand III
            Santa Fe, New Mexico
Design Firm Harry 3
            Muse Design
            Santa Fe, New Mexico

"Space Age" business card for a graphic designer relies on an
unusual typeface and geometric shapes. Printed in three colors
with a vertical orientation, it demands attention.

Client   Johnson Architecture
            Fresno, California
Design Firm Kevin Akers
            San Rafael, California

In a rather deconstructionist form, this business card was created
for an architect. Lines, boxes, circles, and negative elements
give this uniquely die cut card an identity all its own.

Client   Wave Company
             Madison, Wisconsin
Design Firm Z•D Studios, Inc.
             Madison, Wisconsin

Three different business cards were actually printed in only one color. Logo stickers were added to make a series. This is a good idea for saving money because the stickers can be used anywhere to add life to a one-color printing.

David Fleer
Producer△Director

2586 Petersburg Circle
Madison Wisconsin 53719

☎ 608.559.WAVE
📠 608.277.0778

Client   Katie Sullivan
             San Francisco,
             California
Design Firm Shields Design
             Fresno,
             California

A giant fountain pen carried by a little girl is the image on this card for a woman specializing in writing and editing. Printed in two colors, only the pen utilizes this option to create focus.

KATIE SULLIVAN
Writing & Editing

2351 Larkin Street San Francisco, California 94109 415/771-8303

CAROL J. MCCUTCHEON

GENERAL, COSMETIC & FAMILY DENTISTRY

Dr. Carol

CAROL MCCUTCHEON, D.D.S, INC.
621 EAST CAMPBELL AVE. SUITE 18
CAMPBELL, CA 95008
408/379-0851 FAX 378-7515

OPEN SAYS ME!

Client   Carol McCutcheon, DDS
              Campbell, California
Design Firm   A E R I A L
              San Francisco,
                     California

YOU HAVE AN IMPORTANT
DATE WITH DR. CAROL!

ON..

AT..

FOR..

CALL TO CONFIRM! 408/379-0851
621 EAST CAMPBELL AVE. SUITE 18
...MPBELL, CA 95008

IT'S A DATE!

OPEN SAYS ME!

TWICE A DAY

A series of business and
appointment cards for a
dentist's office are printed on
both sides in warm pink and
green. They come in many
shapes and sizes. One side has
all text info. The other side is a
full-bleed, halftone of a woman's
smile with a message in green
printed across it.

Client   Shields Design
             Fresno, California
Design Firm Shields Design
             Fresno, California

The power of design is represented by the image of a giant pencil, secured with chains, lifted by a crane above the city.

Client   Fauxing & Stencils by M.O.M.
             Madison, Wisconsin
Design Firm Z•D Studios, Inc.
             Madison, Wisconsin

Two cards with the same image, but completely different looks because of color application. Stenciled figures and textured background hint at the business.

Client   Metaling in Art
              Houston, Texas
Design Firm   Kelman Design Studio
              Houston, Texas

Metal discs with the company name, all in perspective, are the visual strength of this business card. Inner disc is copper foil stamped. A very striking card, it's printed full-bleed black with reversed text.

Client   Motorhead
              Louisville, Kentucky
Design Firm   Walter McCord & Mary Cawein
                                    Graphic Design
              Louisville, Kentucky

A visual definition of this photography business's name is entitled to half the card's surface, with the address and phone in small caps above.

MICHAEL J. BENZ

**3927 S.GRAND BLVD.
ST.LOUIS, MO 63118**

**314-351-4911
FAX 351-6209**

Client   Benz Print Werks
             St. Louis, Missouri
Design Firm Bartels & Company, Inc.
             St. Louis, Missouri

The logo of this printing company is Swiss/German in feel (and spelling). Very structured with an evident grid, mechanical elements represent a printing press and offer a sense of strength.

Client   Aguilar
             New York, New York
Design Firm Sagmeister Inc.
             New York, New York

Technical imagery succeeds on a business card for an electronic equipment company. Phone number is offered in the format of an electronic dial. The strongest element is the name logo.

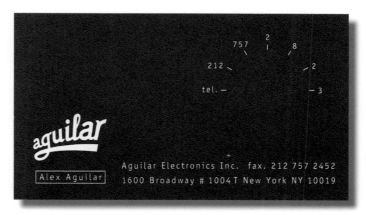

Client   Random Bus
              New York,
                        New York
Design Firm   Sagmeister Inc.
              New York,
                        New York

Random Bus

Telephone 212 355 2227
Facsimile 212 755 1737

305 East 46 Street, New York City, New York, 10017-3058

The bus photographs are the individualizing feature of this music studio's card. One side has the bus coming toward you. Turn the card over and the bus is speeding away—but not before you can call the number.

Client   Eleanor Miller
              Louisville, Kentucky
Design Firm   Walter McCord Graphic Design
              Louisville, Kentucky

Six frames from a "moving picture" walk across the bottom of this producer's card. Sometimes one-color black printing is a compromise to expense, but this business card would have a completely different—and not as successful—effect if printed in color.

Eleanor Bingham Miller   Producer

6408 Longview Lane
Louisville,
Kentucky 40222
502 893 2262

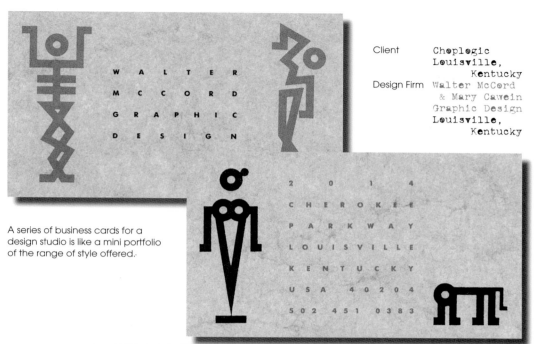

Client   Choplogic
           Louisville,
                Kentucky
Design Firm Walter McCord
           & Mary Cawein
           Graphic Design
           Louisville,
                Kentucky

A series of business cards for a design studio is like a mini portfolio of the range of style offered.

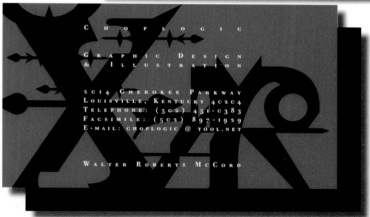

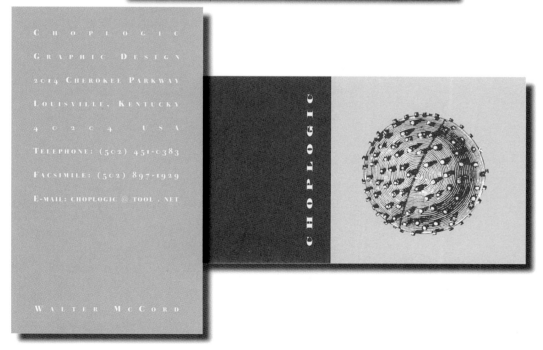

Lonnie R. Posey
Head Master Instructor
4th Degree Black Belt

Classes Daily
Private Lessons Available
Discipline
Honor
Integrity
Perseverence

Families · Groups
Children · Adults

(713) 271-6030

Client   World Champion Karate
              Houston, Texas
Design Firm   Kelman Design Studio
              Houston, Texas

Gold foil stamping works very well with black, but the touch of red adds
visual interest. Card is divided into image and text sections without losing
its entity.

Client   Internet Tool & Die
              Louisville, Kentucky
Design Firm   Walter McCord & Mary Cawein
                              Graphic Design
              Louisville, Kentucky

An intriguing name that almost seems a contradiction in terms is
further represented by a blacksmith against an atomic
background.

INTERNET TOOL & DIE, INC.
BAKERY SQUARE
SUITE NO. 332
120 WEBSTER STREET
LOUISVILLE, KY 40206
TEL: (502) 584-8665
FAX: (502) 585-5005
E-MAIL: BRIAN @ TOOL . NET
WEB: WWW . TOOL . NET

BRIAN SCHAFFNER

Client   Frank's Disaster Art
              Vienna, Austria
Design Firm   Sagmeister Inc.
              New York, New York

Artwork and business name are perfectly integrated. One wonders if the company name is an editorial comment on itself. Frank's Disaster Art deals with automated art-machines.

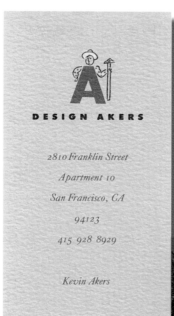

Client   Design Akers
              San Francisco, California
Design Firm   Kevin Akers
              San Rafael, California

Textured tan stock has one deckle edge. Farm theme is carried out on both sides of this business card, playing off the last name of the designer.

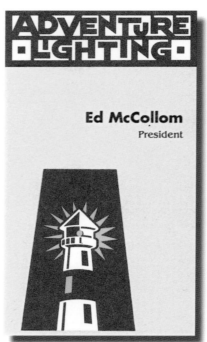

Client   Adventure Lighting
             Des Moines, Iowa
Design Firm Sayles Graphic Design
             Des Moines, Iowa

A lighthouse's golden beam against the navy night is a good logo for a retail lighting company. Graphic illustrative style is repeated from the artwork in the typography of the business name.

Client   Deli Drink Co.
             Atlanta, Georgia
Design Firm Creative Soup, Inc.
             Atlanta, Georgia

Postmark-like logo printed in a watermark fashion hints at travel, faraway places, and exotic drinks. The theme is further enhanced by the diagonally-striped edging on two edges of the card, much like an air mail envelope.

NU MARKET DRINK CO.

P.O. BOX 420947
ATLANTA, GA 30342
PHONE 404•252•5799
FAX 404•250•1287

Deli DRINK CO.

MICHAEL D. ARMSTRONG

KEVIN AKERS

13 HART STREET

SAN RAFAEL, CA

ZIP 94901-2605

HOME 415.459.3424

STUDIO 415.455.0562

FAX 415.455.0597

MODEM 415.459.4767

Client   Kevin Akers
              San Rafael, California
Design Firm   Kevin Akers
              San Rafael, California

A personal calling card looks friendly with an illustration of a home complete with fire in the fireplace and orange tree in the front yard. The card back is printed full bleed sky blue with the orange tree alone. It's later in the season and the fruit is ready to be picked.

Client   TechSource
              Fresno, California
Design Firm   Shields Design
              Fresno, California

A happy Mac adorns the card of a Macintosh sales and service business. A printed textured background is comprised of computer-generated, broken, jaggy lines. They appear embossed in some areas, and above the surface in others by use of shadows.

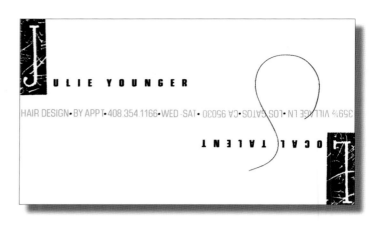

Client   Local Talent
           Los Gatos, California
Design Firm Tharp Did It
           Los Gatos, California

Quite symmetrical business card for haircutters has half of its information readable by one horizontal orientation; the remaining can be read when the card is turned upside down (or right side up). A good job was done on balance with the aid of decorated initial caps, but perfect symmetry is avoided by the employ of a stray hair printed on the card.

Client   Beth Unger
           St. Louis, Missouri
Design Firm CUBE Advertising & Design
           St. Louis, Missouri

Wedding dress designer and seamstress's card starts out with the ever appropriate words, "I do." Unfold the card and get the whole information. Printed black on white, two nice fonts were used in conjunction to create a simplistic elegant look.

"I do."

"I do wedding dres

Beth Unger 314.644.0331

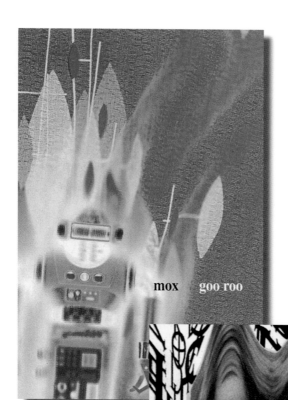

Client   Mox
              San Francisco, California
Design Firm Walter McCord & Mary Cavein
                      Graphic Design
              Louisville, Kentucky

Cards for a recording artist actually look like cassette
liners. Wide variety of styles heightens interest and
leaves you wondering exactly what kind of music
Mox performs.

Client   Sagmeister Inc.
             New York, New York
Design Firm Sagmeister Inc.
             New York, New York

Acetate sleeve provides the arena for a "hands-on" business card. Pulling
one of two cards out of the case creates a most disturbing moire effect,
but what is left is this graphic design firm's information plainly visible in the
lined background's negative space.

Client   Robin Hassett Photography
             Fresno, California
Design Firm Shields Design
             Fresno, California

A woodcut-style image of a photographer robin is the focal
point of this business card. The actual card stock has fibers in it so
a rectangle of white ink was printed and the artwork was printed
onto that. This printing technique makes the art a much stronger
image than to have simply printed it on the untreated stock.

Client   Chicago Dog & Deli
           Des Moines, Iowa
Design Firm Sayles Graphic Design
           Des Moines, Iowa

Stimulating colors suggest excitement and make this vertical card easy to recognize. The back, printed full bleed red with reversed type, is a public relations forum offering information and free food items.

Client   Richard Joel Seidel
           Chicago, Illinois
Design Firm Bartels & Company, Inc.
           St. Louis, Missouri

Printed gray on white, this clothing consultant's card has a bright red thread actually sewn across the center.

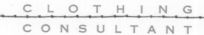

GREATEST

Client John W. Kaufman
     Santa Rosa, California
Design Firm Buttitta Design
     Healdsburg, California

Scribbled silhouette of a horse coming out of a black bar on the
left of the card leaves no surprise that this is for an equine
practice. Scribble texture is repeated more lightly in the background adding to the vitality of the card.

Client The Langsford Center
     Louisville, Kentucky
Design Firm Walter McCord Graphic Design
     Louisville, Kentucky

Anatomical artwork highlights the body parts related to this reading and
learning disorder clinic: mouth, eye, ear. Art is in gray, type in black on
cream. Text is printed in small caps. Specific information is found on the flip
side.

THE LANGSFORD CENTER
LEARNING TO EXCEL

CLAUDIA R. CHERVENAK, DIRECTOR

THE BELKNAP BUILDING . 1810 SILS AVENUE
LOUISVILLE, KENTUCKY 40205 . TEL: 502 473.7000

Client   Global-Dining, Inc.
              Tokyo, Japan
Design Firm   Vrontikis Design Office
              Los Angeles, California

Two companion business cards are similarly executed, but differ in a couple of ways. One is printed in Japanese, the other English. Different views of the world on respective cards combine to show as much of the world as can possibly be seen at one time—which is really only half.

Client   Holocaust Museum Houston
              Houston, Texas
Design Firm   Kelman Design Studio
              Houston, Texas

A rather somber card, this is printed in black on white. It contains wonderfully executed artwork full of symbolism, not the least of which is a partial star of David in negative space.

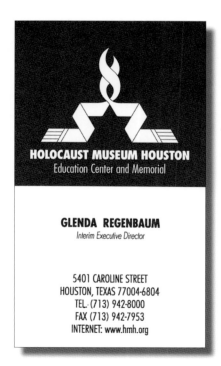

Client   Van-Michael Salon
              Atlanta, Georgia
Design Firm   Creative Soup, Inc.
              Atlanta, Georgia

Metallic mauve ink and lingerie clad halftone make no mistake that this salon targets women. Distinctive mix of fonts and type sizes work well as an additional graphic element.

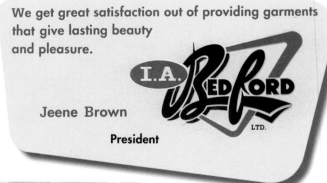

Client   I.A Bedford
              Des Moines, Iowa
Design Firm   Sayles Graphic
                      Design
              Des Moines, Iowa

Original card shape repeats an element from this fabric manufacturer's logo. The entire logo is embossed and printed on the business card front. On the back are phone numbers and address on a full bleed paisley background.

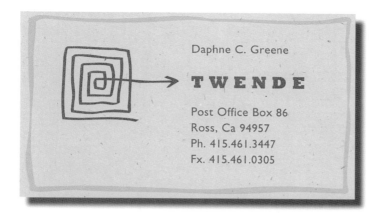

Client   Twende
              Ross, California
Design Firm Kevin Akers
              San Rafael,
              California

Third World travel guide business
card would appeal to one who likes
to go "outside the box". Simple,
flowing graphics on tan card stock is
faintly indicative of the cultures
waiting to be experienced. On the
back, the Swahili word "Twende" is
defined.

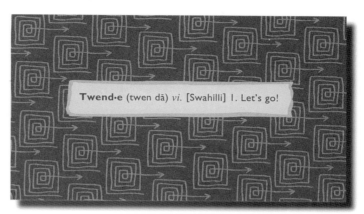

Client   Heritage Plaza Mortgage, Inc.
              Clovis, California
Design Firm Shields Design
              Fresno, California

Concentrating on the area in which this mortgage company is located
sets a tone of stability and longevity. Note the art deco font from the
same period in which many of the skyscrapers were built.

BEVERLY ST. CLAIR BAIRD
MANAGING DIRECTOR

2 JENNER STREET
SUITE 150
IRVINE, CA 92718
PHONE: 714/727-4211
FAX: 714/727-4217

DISCOVER TODAY'S MOTORCYCLING

Client   Motorcycle Industry Council
              Irvine, California
Design Firm   Kevin Akers
              San Rafael, California

If this motorcycle marketing group's goal was to introduce a kinder,
gentler biker image to the general population, the card is a success. In
magenta and green, the free-form figures on wheels appear to be taking
a leisurely ride on one of America's gently curving roads. Upon close
examination, the figures look like they're wearing helmets.

Client   Rae Simonini Hildreth
              Des Moines, Iowa
Design Firm   Sayles Graphic Design
              Des Moines, Iowa

Magenta ink and arrow graphics are worth noting. Actual arrows
with reversed type, an arrow shape in the "A" of the cardholder's
name, even the shape of the card itself are all repeated forms. The
back of the business card is used as an appointment card with a
full bleed "perm" texture background.

YOUR NEXT APPOINTMENT WITH RAE IS:

_____

HAIR DESIGNER · NAIL TECHNICIAN

THE UPPER CUT
118 FIFTH STREET
VALLEY JUNCTION
WEST DES MOINES
255-0704
276-9084

RAE
SIMONINI
HILDRETH

Client   Premier Events
              Deborah Merga
              Santa Rosa, California
Design Firm Buttitta Design
              Healdsburg, California

Bright colors and angled graphics indicate a card for a business full of activity, an event coordinator. The lively logo "P" is reminiscent of party streamers.

Client   Delaney Matrix
              Fresno, California
Design Firm Shields Design
              Fresno, California

The logo of this marketing and advertising firm is enlarged, screened, and repeated in part which gives it the effect of an elegant watermark.

Client   Mr. Reynolds Limousine Service
               Des Moines, Iowa
Design Firm Sayles Graphic Design
               Des Moines, Iowa

Bold black graphics on white stock make a striking card. Folding business
card has a nice unification with artwork and type.

WHO IS MR. REYNOLDS? HE'S YOUR CHAUFFEUR! THE REYNOLDS FAMILY IS COMMITTED TO YOUR SATISFACTION. WE PROMISE IMPECCABLE SERVICE AND A CLEAN STRETCH LIMOUSINE EVERY TIME!

Chuck Crane
PRESIDENT

333 S.W. 5th Street ◆ Grants Pass, Oregon 97526
503-955-2885 ◆ Fax: 503-955-2889

Client   United States Chart Company
              Grants Pass, Oregon
Design Firm   Shields Design
              Fresno, California

Full color logo with historical and chartmaking tools suggest a great
company history—especially when located in a place like Grants Pass.

Client   Community Housing & Services
              Madison, Wisconsin
Design Firm   Z·D Studios, Inc.
              Madison, Wisconsin

Nice imagery for a nonprofit housing provider: upward stairs,
sunshine, and homes. Printed with black ink one feels the cost was
reasonably modest and maybe the housing provider knows the
value of a buck; the design of the card is excellent so quality
matters, too.

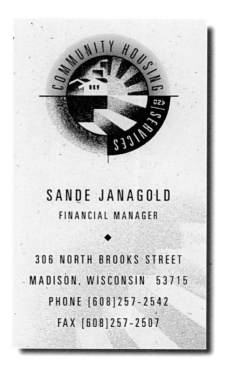

Client   Color Express
              Newark, California
Design Firm   Kevin Akers
              San Rafael, California

Big swashes of color make a statement on this card for car paint
distributors. It's printed in four colors of ink, but the expressive style
of the graphics makes registration unnecessary.

Doug Walker
Director

HEAD FIRST

1408 De Porres Lane

St. Charles, MO 63303

314-926-3861

Client   Head First
              St. Charles, Missouri
Design Firm   Bartels & Company, Inc.
              St. Louis, Missouri

Helmeted figure is part of a very strong image, which includes
neon colors and reversed type, for a head injury prevention
charity.

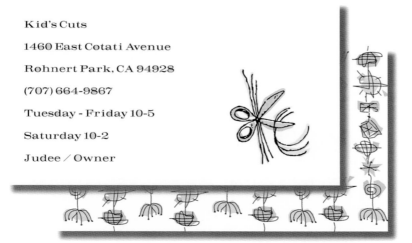

Kid's Cuts

1460 East Cotati Avenue

Rohnert Park, CA 94928

(707) 664-9867

Tuesday - Friday 10-5

Saturday 10-2

Judee / Owner

Client   Kid's Cuts
              Rohnert Park, California
Design Firm   Kevin Akers
              San Rafael, California

kid's cuts

1460 east cotati avenue

rohnert park, ca 94928

(707) 664-9867

tuesday - friday 10-5

saturday 10-2

judee / owner

A variety of very colorful cards is obviously aimed at the clientele of a hair salon that specializes in children. All cards are printed on both sides, typography is freer than most, and the owner is listed by first name only.

kid's cuts

1460 east cotati avenue

rohnert park, ca 94928

(707) 664-9867

tuesday - friday 10-5

saturday 10-2

judee / owner

Client   Lou Freeman
                      Photography
              Atlanta, Georgia
Design Firm Creative Soup, Inc.
              Atlanta, Georgia

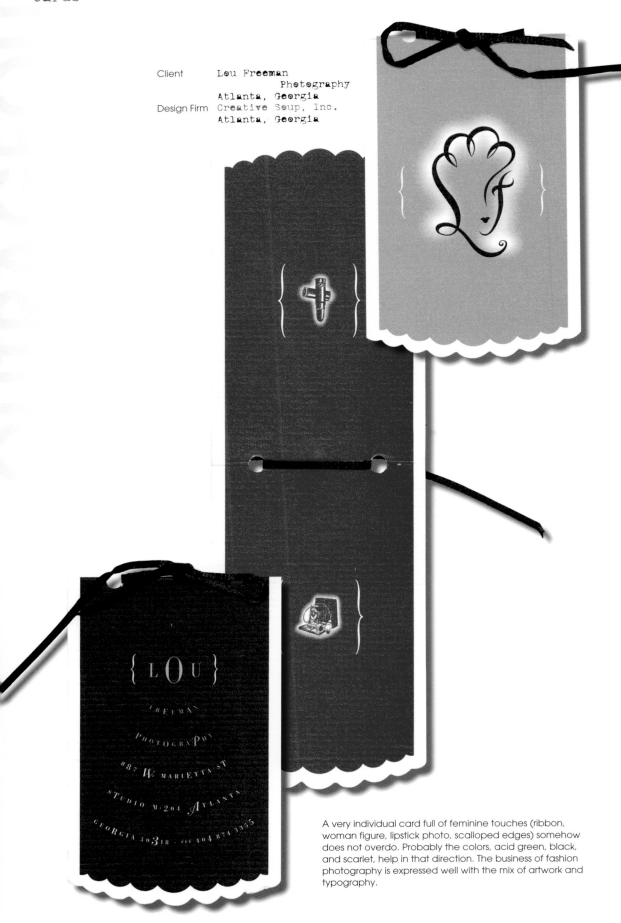

A very individual card full of feminine touches (ribbon, woman figure, lipstick photo, scalloped edges) somehow does not overdo. Probably the colors, acid green, black, and scarlet, help in that direction. The business of fashion photography is expressed well with the mix of artwork and typography.

Client Martin Chair, Inc.
     New Holland, Pennsylvania
Design Firm Dean Design/Marketing Group, Inc.
     Lancaster, Pennsylvania

CHARLES E. MARTIN

SALES MANAGER

124 KING COURT

NEW HOLLAND

PENNSYLVANIA

· 17557

PHONE

717 / 355 / 2177

717 / 354 / 9176

FAX

717 / 355 / 2351

From Rt. 23: 1.3 miles south on
Diller Ave. in New Holland.

From Rt. 340: 3.5 miles north on
Hollander Rd. in Intercourse.

Showroom Hours:
Mon.–Fri. 9–5
Thurs. 9–8
Sat. 9–4

Handcrafted wood furniture is reflected on this folded business
card. The front has a woodcut-style logo of a carpenter at a lathe,
and silhouette of a chair back. Inside has woodcut style wood grain
printed with a three-sided bleed on half the card, while the other
half has all pertinent information. The back of the card has added
features of a map and driving directions which are both great for
out-of-town customers.

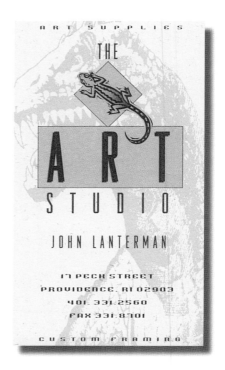

Client   Art Studio
             Providence, Rhode Island
Design Firm Adkins/Balchunas
             Pawtucket, Rhode Island

Reptilian imagery dominates this business card for a retail art
supplies store. A tyrannical dinosaur is the screened background,
while the foreground offers a much calmer iguana second in
dominance only to the word "ART".

Client   La Boulangerie
             Fresno, California
Design Firm Shields Design
             Fresno, Calfornia

A comforting illustration of hot beverage and freshly baked
bread sets a welcoming tone for a French bakery & cafe. The
same image is enlarged and printed in part, in reverse and one
color, at the bottom the card.

Client   Des Moines
                    Plumbing
              Des Moines, Iowa
Design Firm   Sayles Graphic
                    Design
              Des Moines, Iowa

Blue and yellow are printed on gray.
Strong illustrative graphics are
highlighted by the plumbing lines
which act as dividers for information
cells.

Client   Attitude Online
              Fresno, California
Design Firm   Shields Design
              Fresno, California

The name logo of this internet service provider mixes lower and
uppercase letters, and even has a ligature. The lightning bolt held
by the figure is enlarged and repeated across the card, bleeding
off two sides.

St. Louis Cosmetic Surgery, Inc.

Bruce I. White, M.D.
Certified American Board
of Plastic Surgery

456 N. New Ballas Rd., Suite 211

St. Louis, Mo 63141

(314) 569-2030 *(24 hrs.)*

Client   St. Louis Cosmetic Surgery
             St. Louis, Missouri
Design Firm Bartels & Company, Inc.
             St. Louis, Missouri

Excellent embossing of a rough, aged, skin texture fading into beautiful, smooth skin—the kind of skin you'd like to have.

Client   Hank's Cheesecakes
             St. Louis, Missouri
Design Firm Bartels & Company, Inc.
             St. Louis, Missouri

Wonderful example of a logo with an art deco flavor employs a repeated curve that very nearly composes a half circle. Background colors are subtle. Different, but from the same color family, these hues provide a softening tone to the logo.

HALSTED
COMMUNICATIONS
INC.

BLAINE MALLORY
ASSOCIATE.

FONE
800.600.7111
X228
FAX
800.600.7112
E-MAIL
HALSTED@IX.NETCOM.COM

Client   Halsted
            Communications
            Los Angeles,
                California
Design Firm Vrontikis
                Design Office
            Los Angeles,
                California

44 MONTGOMERY ST.
SUITE 3055
SAN FRANCISCO, CA 94104

555 CAPITOL MALL
SUITE 430
SACRAMENTO, CA 95814

1330 AVE OF THE AMERICAS
24TH FLOOR
NEW YORK, NY 10019

1301 CONNECTICUT AVE.
7TH FLOOR
WASHINGTON, D.C. 20036

56 E. MAIN ST.
SUITE 200
VENTURA, CA 93001

ARCO TOWER
515 SOUTH FLOWER ST.
SUITE 700
LOS ANGELES, CA 90071

THE AVENTINE
8910 UNIVERSITY CTR.
SUITE 300
SAN DIEGO, CA 92122

BLAINE MALLORY
ASSOCIATE.

FONE
800.600.7111
X228
FAX
800.600.7112
E-MAIL
HALSTED@IX.NETCOM.COM

Disseminating a lot of information can be a real challenge with respect to the limited space on a typical business card. The solution here was to create a flap. When it's closed, the uncluttered card offers logo, names, and numbers. For a list of several addresses, open the flap. The back of the card is printed full bleed with a muted, enlarged partial version of the logo.

Client   Corinne Antipa
            Santa Rosa,
                California
Design Firm Buttitta Design
            Healdsburg,
                California

Free-spirited logo visually speaks of unencumbered movement which is exactly what this Feldenkrais practitioner offers.

FELDENKRAIS METHOD
*A dynamic approach
for achieving your
movement potential*

. . . .

CORINNE ANTIPA
Feldenkrais Practitioner
707 538-8543

Client   Raccoon River Brewing Company
              Des Moines, Iowa
Design Firm   Sayles Graphic Design
              Des Moines, Iowa

Die cut card accents the raccoon illustration for this restaurant and brew pub. The back of the card is gray and black raccoon striped.

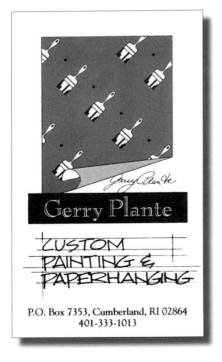

Client   Gerry Plante
              Cumberland, Rhode Island
Design Firm   Adkins/Balchunas
              Pawtucket, Rhode Island

In order to reinforce the idea that this painting and paperhanging is custom done, different techniques were employed. The service offered is hand lettered. A pattern of paintbrushes was used on a strip of wallpaper in the process of being hung. The final touch is the business owner's name written as an artist's signature at the bottom of his work.

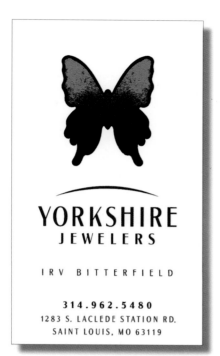

YORKSHIRE
J E W E L E R S

IRV BITTERFIELD

314.962.5480
1283 S. LACLEDE STATION RD.
SAINT LOUIS, MO 63119

Client   Yorkshire Jewelers
              St. Louis, Missouri
Design Firm   Bartels & Company, Inc.
              St. Louis, Missouri

As it rises above the horizon, the color application in this butterfly is interesting. Fading from blue to black, it's not the least bit hard-edged, but in fact looks smeared, smudged, spattered, and even has a twill effect in some areas.

CUSTOM SAFETY FLOOR MATTING

sbemco
INTERNATIONAL, INC.
10392 RALEIGH RD. ST. PAUL, MN 55129

MARK TUCCI
National Accounts Manager

CUSTOMER SERVICE   TEL. (612)730-1897
(800)468-0860   FAX. (612)730-1912

Client   Sbemco
              Des Moines,
                        Iowa
Design Firm   Sayles
              Graphic Design
              Des Moines,
                        Iowa

Magenta, cyan, and black always make an eye-catching combination. The back of this card is printed full bleed with a very realistic floor mat (what the company makes) texture. Incorporated into the texture is a partial company logo.

A STEP AHEAD

Client   Phantom Incorporated
              St. Louis, Missouri
Design Firm   Bartels & Company, Inc.
              St. Louis, Missouri

Highly unusual card for a manufacturer of automotive accessories,
but the generation that would find appealing the theme of a
cartoon, action hero is the same generation who grew up
dreaming of hot rods and cool cars.

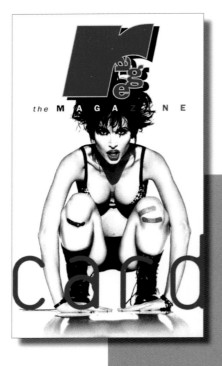

Client   Larry Flint/Rage
              Beverly Hills, California
Design Firm   Mike Salisbury Communications Inc.
              Torrance, California

Blood red and acid green, staggered and stacked
typography, and the girl you won't be bringing home to
Mother (or even you best friend's apartment) all
contribute to the attitude of an angry, offensive,
in-your-face card that represents its business well.

JAMIE SHEEHAN
2505 SECOND AVE #700
SEATTLE WA 98121
PH FX 206 448 2651

Client   Sheehan Design
              Seattle, Washington
Design Firm   Sheehan Design
              Seattle, Washington

Phonetic rebus makes it known that design is all important. Neon yellow swirls are a fun visual game if there's the least bit of astigmatism present.

Client   Radical Concepts Inc.
              Menlo Park, California
Design Firm   Russell Leong Design
              Palo Alto, California

Sunglassed, bright green frog sitting on his Rad Pad makes a humorous and memorable symbol for this company whose business is bean bag chairs.

RADICAL CONCEPTS INC.

STEVE PEARSON
EXECUTIVE VICE PRESIDENT

945 HAMILTON AVENUE
MENLO PARK, CA 94025
T 415.328.9600
F 415.328.9601
spearson@radconcepts.com

Client   Pacific Coast Builders
             Huntington Beach, California
Design Firm Billy Goats Gruff
             Encinitas, California

The layout of this business card is very Mondrian-esque, an artistic but
appropriate choice for a construction company. Also well-suited for a
construction company, but very unMondrian, is the color scheme of
earthy and neutral tones. Card is printed with a full bleed, front and back,
with all type reversed in white.

Client   Racine Danish Kringles
             Racine, Wisconsin
Design Firm Becker Design
             Milwaukee, Wisconsin

This is a nice logo that might have been boring, but not with repeated
shapes, a flourish, and ligature or two. Logo is enlarged, screened, and
printed in part as a background for the business card.

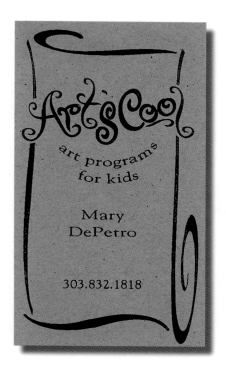

Client   Art's Cool
            Mary DePetro
            Denver, Colorado
Design Firm Ellen Bruss Design
            Denver, Colorado

Low budget does not mean bad design. This card for an arts program for inner city children is full of flowing lines and fun type on darker than usual stock. Everything about it speaks to its purpose.

Client   Donald MacNair
            Santa Rosa, California
Design Firm Buttitta Design
            Healdsburg, California

Fall leaves, gradating from a pale peach to a rich red orange on a dark green gray background, are a striking symbol for a landscape architect. Realistic in feel, a wonderful texture is created when the negative space around and behind the leaves invades their color.

Client   Cutler Travel
              Marketing
        West Des
              Moines, Iowa
Design Firm Sayles Graphic
              Design
        Des Moines,
              Iowa

Soft green and violet make a
pleasing palette for this travel
marketing firm. Strong graphics on
the front, and superimposed on
the company initials on the back,
make it plain what the business is
about.

Client   Stratford Publishing
        Tucson, Arizona
Design Firm Boelts Bros., Associates
        Tucson, Arizona

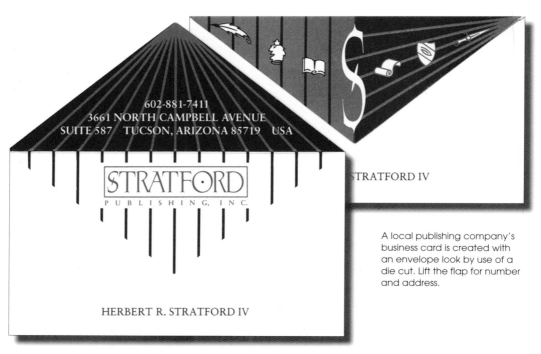

A local publishing company's
business card is created with
an envelope look by use of a
die cut. Lift the flap for number
and address.

Client   Wave Property
              Management
              Cedarburg,
              Wisconsin
Design Firm   Becker Design
              Milwaukee,
              Wisconsin

Very clean card employs an icon printed in metallic copper. The verbal equivalent is also printed in metallic copper with the rest of the text in teal. Card stock is subtly different colors on either side.

Lance Lichter
President

W62 N551
Washington Ave.
Cedarburg, WI
53012

414.375.6868 *p*
414.375.6869 *f*

Client   Jeff Greenburg/Village
              Hollywood, California
Design Firm   Mike Salisbury
              Communications Inc.
              Torrance, California

A closed door begs to be opened. When it is, information about this recording studio is found inside.

The Village
1616
Butler Avenue
West Los Angeles CA
90025
PHONE 310. 478. 8227
FAX 310. 479. 1142
E-MAIL villagerec@aol.com

Julie Hormel
President

Client   Goodtime Jazz Festival
              Des Moines, Iowa
Design Firm   Sayles Graphic Design
              Des Moines, Iowa

Printed on one side very much like a concert ticket, this business card was
made for a jazz festival organizer. Period illustrations and typography are
reminiscent of the height-of-jazz era.

Client   Julian Haro
              Eugene, Oregon
Design Firm   Lincoln Design
              Eugene, Oregon

An initial letter logo found in the trailing thread from a needle is the focus
of this business card for a master tailor. Note that the thread goes through
the letter "o" at the end of the last name.

JUSTIN'S SEATTLE
ESPRESSO & ITALIAN SODA

Jeff Woon

3-62-102
Nishimiyashita
Ageo-Shi Saitama-Ken
362 Japan
Tel. 048-776-6723
Fax 048-553-3037

ジャスティンズ
シアトル

エスプレッソ コーヒー
イタリアン ソーダ

ジェフ ウォーン

〒362 埼玉県上尾市西宮下3-62-102

TEL (048) 776-6723

FAX (0485) 53-3037

アメリカ トラニ シロップ 日本代理店

Client   Justin's
              Japan
Design Firm Gable Design Group
              Seattle, Washington

The colors of the Italian flag (green, white, and red) are an integral part of the design for this espresso and Italian soda bar's business card. It's printed in English on one side, Japanese on the other.

Client   Mike Salisbury Communications
              Torrance, California
Design Firm Mike Salisbury Communications Inc.
              Torrance, California

Being able to incorporate past work into a business card is like carrying a mini portfolio. It's difficult to execute for many reasons, space restrictions among the rest, but this design was a great success.

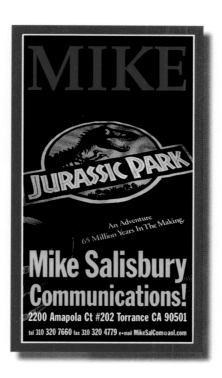

MIKE

JURASSIC PARK

An Adventure
65 Million Years In The Making.

Mike Salisbury
Communications!
2200 Amapola Ct #202 Torrance CA 90501
tel 310 320 7660 fax 310 320 4779 e-mail MikeSalCom@aol.com

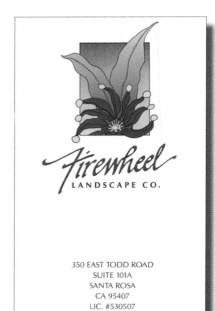

Client   **Firewheel Landscape Co.**
            Santa Rosa, California
Design Firm **Buttitta Design**
            Healdsburg, California

Exotic-looking plant somehow seems to echo the name of this landscape company. Printed in three colors, a variety of shades and mixes were created with gradient screens. Calligraphic logo and illustration coordinate very well.

Client   **Monsoon Cafe**
            Santa Monica, California
Design Firm **Vrontikis Design Office**
            Los Angeles, California

The name of this Asian eclectic restaurant is the focus of the graphics on this business card. Swirling strokes are integral, with the logo typography mimicking the same shape and technique. Back of card is printed with the full bleed image of a pale yellow vortex.

Client   Design Milwaukee
              Milwaukee, Wisconsin
Design Firm   Becker Design
              Milwaukee, Wisconsin

Typographic logo dominates both sides of business card for a not-for-profit design society. On one side, the logo is reversed out of a pale olive green background. On the flip, the logo itself is printed in pale olive green. Both logos bleed off the top and left side of the card. Other information is printed across.

Client   Baldini's
              Boston, Massachusetts
Design Firm   Adkins/Balchunas
              Pawtucket, Rhode Island

First and foremost the business name attracts attention. Its printed large and in bright colors. Green and red are often indicative of things Italian as is the case with this card for a pizza chain. Sketches of tomatoes and peppers suggest fresh vegetables are used in the cooking while the images themselves balance each other as design elements.

G REGORY
McC LATCHY
FILM

8918 SANTA MONICA BLVD

WEST HOLLYWOOD

CA   90069

310.854.3922
FAX   310.854.3925

Client   Greg McClatchy Films
              West Hollywood, California
Design Firm   Mike Salisbury Communications Inc.
              Torrance, California

This typographic logo at first glance doesn't appear typographic,
just a very interesting combination of angles and geometric
shapes. Sans serif font compliments this design strongly influenced
by the Bauhaus.

Client   Axia
              Los Angeles & San Francisco, California
Design Firm   Vrontikis Design Office
              Los Angeles, California

Binary language, computer screen, jaggy printing are all included in the
logo for this company whose business is new media design. Purple and
rusty orange create the complementary color scheme. Card is smaller
than most, and printed full bleed on the back with binary code screened
in.

san francisco & los angeles

petrula vrontikis
creative director

axia

2021 pontius avenue los angeles california 90025
ph310.478.4775   fax310.478.4685   e-mailpvaxia@vdo.com

Client   Tucson Arts District
              Tucson, Arizona
Design Firm Boelts Bros., Associates
              Tucson, Arizona

Considering the geographic location of this local arts coalition, the design of its card is appropriately influenced by Southwestern art. From the patterned bar that bleeds off the left of the card, a hand throws a purple star into the air. Besides the bullets in the address, it's the only colored element in the design.

Client   Jeff Greene
              Sebastopol, California
Design Firm Buttitta Design
              Healdsburg, California

"Martial arts for peace" is successfully repeated in the design of this card. Soft gray purple and cool green are very calming colors. Full of Oriental imagery, the calligraphic typography completes a design that relates in every way.

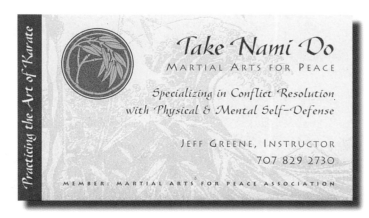

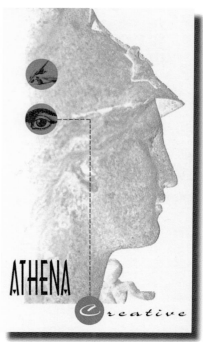
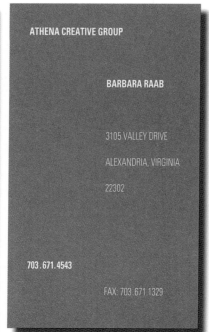

Client   Athena Creative
            Alexandria, Virginia
Design Firm Barbara Raab Design
            Alexandria, Virginia

What better image for a firm named "Athena" than the goddess herself? Back of card is printed full bleed green with reversed text.

Client   Miami County Urologists
            Troy, Ohio
Design Firm 1-earth GRAPHICS
            Troy, Ohio

Graphics leave little doubt that the business card is utilized by urologists. Interesting to think that some years ago these drawings might have been deemed vulgar. Now they're practically iconic. Cards were printed with both horizontal and vertical orientations.

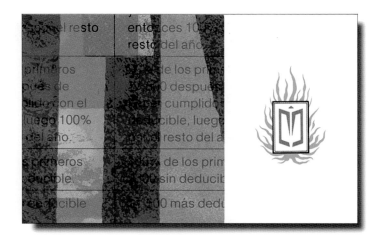

Client   Margo Chase
                 Design
           Los Angeles,
               California

Design Firm   Margo Chase
                 Design
           Los Angeles,
               California

Outside of business card is a collage printed with a variety of inks—very busy, but a good design. Open the card and find a completely different atmosphere. Printed with only three inks, the inside has lots of white space and is easy to read.

maRgo
CHASE
design

2 2 5 5
BANCROFT
AVENUE
los angeles
CA 90039

Client   Snowden & Roy
           Boca Raton, Florida

Design Firm   Adkins/Balchunas
           Pawtucket, Rhode Island

Incorporating Classical and Renaissance art that includes linen images was a wonderful choice for this fine linens and antique importer.

165 TOWNSEND STREET
SAN FRANCISCO, CA 94107
FAX: 415.541.7919
415.541.7903

RICHARDSON   ■ ▲ ● ⬠   [ARCHITECTS]

MICHAEL LARKIN, AIA
Architect

Client   Richardson
              San Francisco, California
Design Firm   Russell Leong Design
              Palo Alto, California

Architectural firm's wide card uses copper foil stamping and lots of white space.

Client   LG Interiors
              Bellevue, Washington
Design Firm   Greg Welsh Design
              Seattle, Washington

Much like a fabric sample book, this interior designer's card utilizes die cuts, a rivet, and
extra-heavy stock for a very unique result.

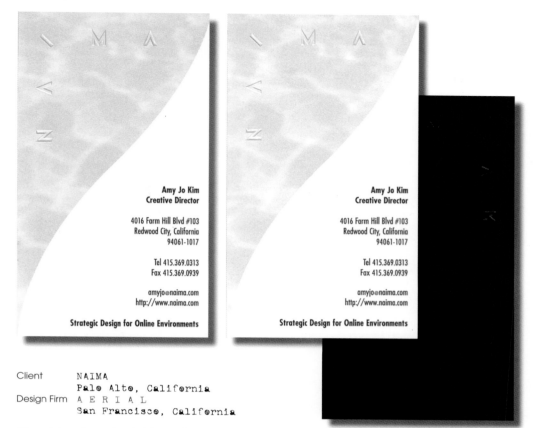

Client   NAIMA
              Palo Alto, California
Design Firm   AERIAL
              San Francisco, California

Alternately embossed and debossed letters make an unusual logo as it wraps itself around the upper left corner of this business card. Gentle curve of ethereal texture softens hard angles of typography. A series of similar cards were printed: some with gray, some with tan, some with full bleed navy backs.

Client   Gerald A. Emanuel
              San Jose, California
Design Firm   AERIAL
              San Francisco, California

Elegant and professional attorney's card has a large script initial blind embossed into the business card. Remaining card is white and printed with navy ink.

LENOX
R O O M

FRANZ STUHLPFARRER

1278 THIRD AVENUE   NEW YORK CITY   10021
TEL 212.772.0404   FAX 212.772.3229
WWW.LENOXROOM.COM

Client   Lenox Room
              New York, New York
Design Firm   A E R I A L
              San Francisco, California

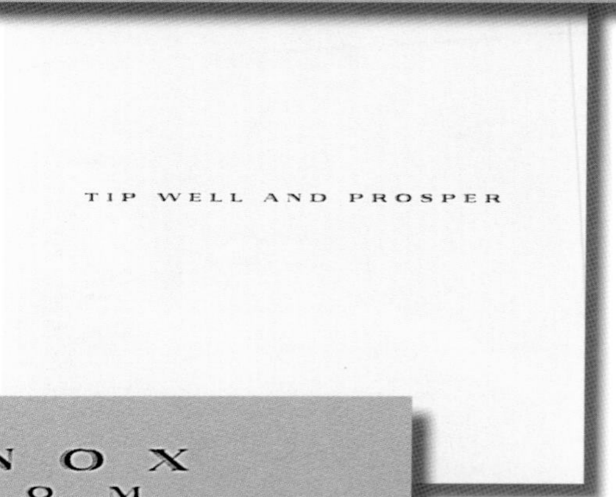

TIP WELL AND PROSPER

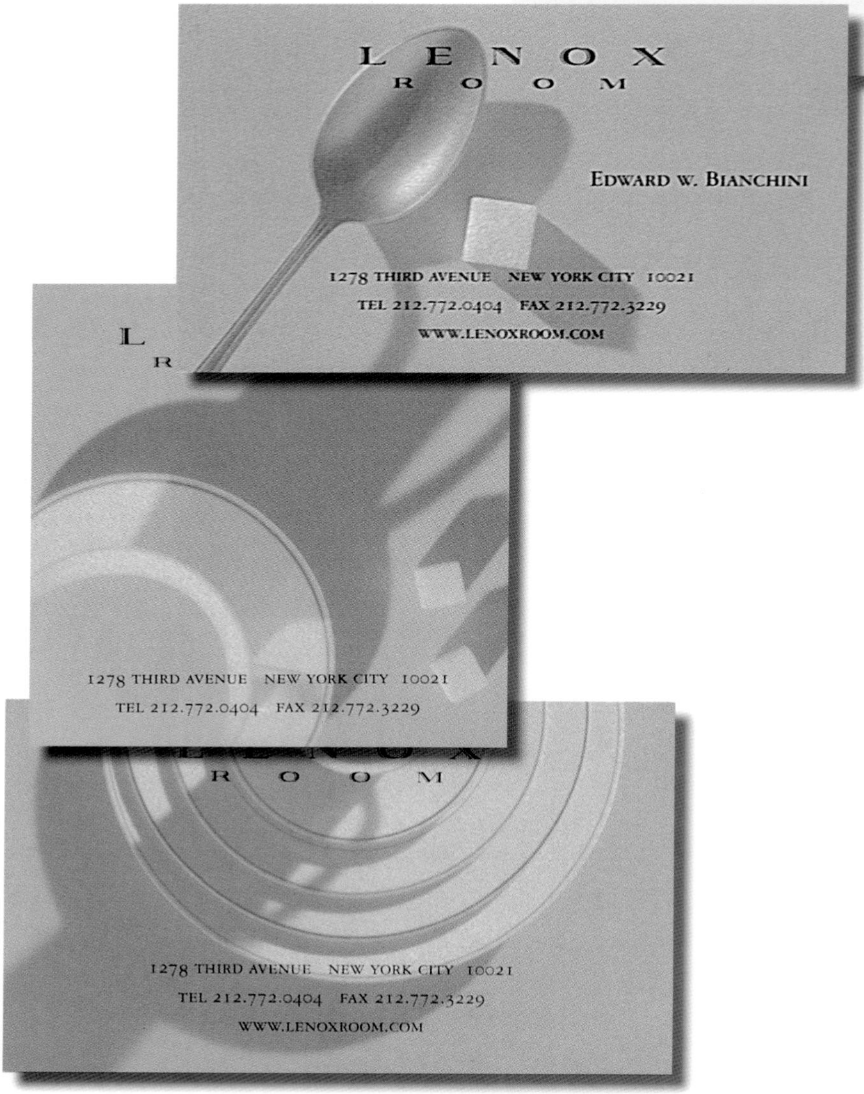

LENOX
R O O M

EDWARD W. BIANCHINI

1278 THIRD AVENUE   NEW YORK CITY   10021
TEL 212.772.0404   FAX 212.772.3229
WWW.LENOXROOM.COM

L
R

1278 THIRD AVENUE   NEW YORK CITY   10021
TEL 212.772.0404   FAX 212.772.3229

LENOX
R O O M

1278 THIRD AVENUE   NEW YORK CITY   10021
TEL 212.772.0404   FAX 212.772.3229
WWW.LENOXROOM.COM

Monochromatic card series is replete with elegant table setting imagery—wonderful shadowed photography. The square cards have a tag line on the back.

Jerry L. McMullin
President

Intelligent Wireless Solutions

P.O. Box 692005-305
Houston, Texas 77269-2005

Phone: 281-356-5689
Fax: 281-356-8274
www.inwireless.com

Client   Intelligent Wireless Solutions
             Houston, Texas
Design Firm Kelman Design Studio
             Houston, Texas

The artwork on this card gives pause to wonder about symbolism. A ball
inside a cube has a very authentic three-dimensional effect by the use of
well-placed gradients. Black and bronze are good color choices.

Client   David Zach Futurist
             Milwaukee, Wisconsin
Design Firm Becker Design
             Milwaukee, Wisconsin

Great visual from the name "Futurist" is a graphic rendering of a Saturn-
type figure, except that the rings don't just go around and around and
around. They come from behind, swirl around and go up. Same symbol is
enlarged and printed full bleed on the back of the card.

Innovative Futures

DAVID ZACH futurist

225 E. St. Paul Avenue
Suite 303
Milwaukee, WI 53202

Phone
414.278.0414
Fax
414.223.4757
E-mail
DMZach@aol.com

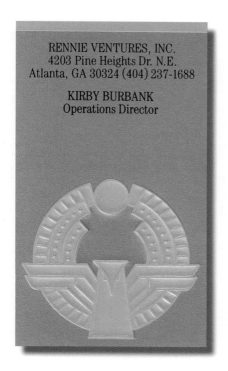

RENNIE VENTURES, INC.
4203 Pine Heights Dr. N.E.
Atlanta, GA 30324 (404) 237-1688

KIRBY BURBANK
Operations Director

Client   **Rennie Ventures, Inc.**
               Atlanta, Georgia
Design Firm **Bartels & Company, Inc.**
               St. Louis, Missouri

Gold foil, metallic ink, and gold foil embossing were chosen for this nightclub operator's card. Of course it hints at a little flash, but is executed in such a way that it offers a feeling of substance.

Client   **Green City**
               New York, New York
Design Firm **Sagmeister Inc.**
               New York, New York

What great symbolism for a business that offers gardening for roof terraces. The Empire State Building casts a tree-shaped shadow. The city and nature don't have to be incompatible.

GREEN CITY

Alexander Gröger

718 599 4867

65 South 8th St. #4
Brooklyn, NY 11211

Client   San Diego State University
                               Ice Hockey Team
             San Diego, California
Design Firm Billy Goats Gruff
             Encinitas, California

Business card for ice hockey team management still has
the obligatory mascot, but it's printed in a unique way:
enlarged, in part, and bleeding off two sides of the card.
Really, this allows for a bigger effect than if the entire logo
were used. Back is printed full bleed black.

Client   David Freedman
             Los Angeles, California
Design Firm Billy Goats Gruff
             Encinitas, California

Tutor of American Sign Language has the initials of his service spelled out
in sign using illustrations of hands. Text fits nicely into the frame formed by
the illustrations. Back is printed full bleed black.

Client   Country Pride
                Denver, Pennsylvania
Design Firm Dean Design/Marketing Group, Inc.
                Lancaster, Pennsylvania

Casual card for a bar-b-que restaurant has an illustration of "Newton" the anthropomorphic chef pig (or is that pig chef) ready to serve another delicious meal. The back of card has an optional fill-in-the-blank for complimentary items. Printed in one color, screens aid in visual interest.

Client   Tharp Did It
                San Francisco,
                      California
Design Firm Tharp Did It
                Los Gatos,
                      California

Two cards with the similar informational fronts have different illustrative backs to which any designer can relate. One is a caricature getting a great idea out of the trash. The other is almost an editorial cartoon (that is more fact than editorial) portraying the computer as angel and devil.

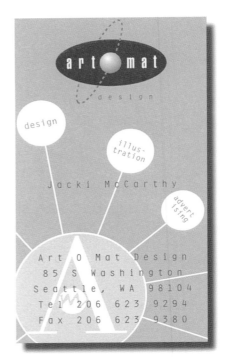

Client   Art O Mat Design
              Seattle, Washington
Design Firm   Art O Mat Design
              Seattle, Washington

Design of business card for design and marketing firm makes
great use of the "O" in company name. Graphics bleed off the
card and typography is superimposed over artwork. Screens and
gradients were employed to get the most color effect for a two-
color printing.

Client   IMI New Ventures
              San Francisco, California
Design Firm   Oh Boy, A Design Company
              San Francisco, California

Three cards are printed with text on one side, leaving lots of white space.
Flip the card over to find the logo reversed out of one of three different full
bleed colors.

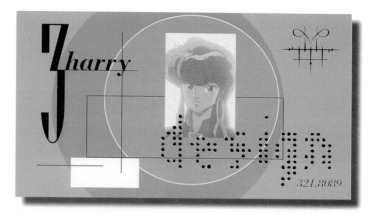

Client   Harry
                  MacDonald
            Forehand III
            Santa Fe,
                  New Mexico
Design Firm Harry3
            Muse Design
            Santa Fe,
                  New Mexico

Two cards for the same design firm are quite different, but have the same futuristic feel. Some of the same imagery was used: figure, color, dots, thin lines. One, however, highlights the design firm while the other concentrates on the designer.

Client   Billy Goats Gruff
            Encinitas, California
Design Firm Billy Goats Gruff
            Encinitas, California

Though I thought the Billy Goats Gruff lived under a bridge, the silhouette here shows one atop a mountain—a better symbol for a business. Rich autumn hues of brown, orange, and green are a very nice color scheme. Both sides are printed full bleed, and both carry strong, but freely-rendered, graphics and type.

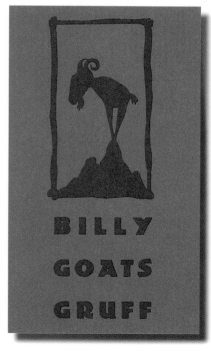

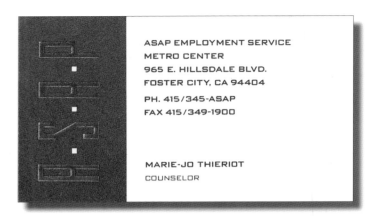

ASAP EMPLOYMENT SERVICE
METRO CENTER
965 E. HILLSDALE BLVD.
FOSTER CITY, CA 94404

PH. 415/345-ASAP

FAX 415/349-1900

MARIE-JO THIERIOT
COUNSELOR

Client   A.S.A.P.
            Foster City, California
Design Firm Kevin Akers
            San Rafael, California

Good name for an employment agency is turned on its side, embossed
and copper foil stamped. The rest of the card is printed in forest green on
white.

Client   Z•D Studios, Inc.
            Madison, Wisconsin
Design Firm Z•D Studios, Inc.
            Madison, Wisconsin

Part of this graphic design firm's logo consistently
uses an angled die cut to aid in the impression of
a turned down corner. Folded business card
atypically opens from the right. Back of card is
printed full bleed with monochromatic photo.

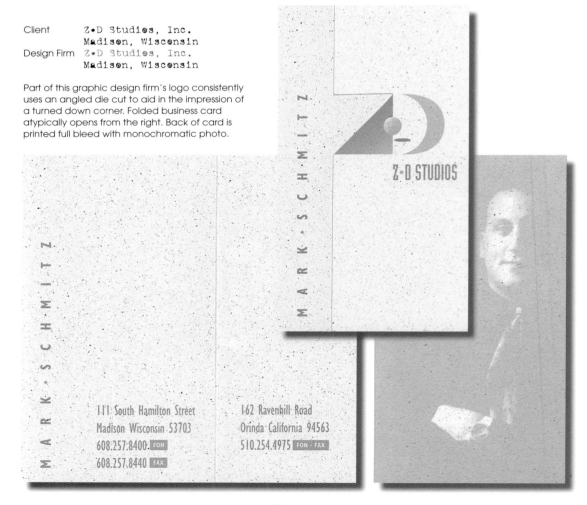

MARK·SCHMITZ

Z•D STUDIOS

111 South Hamilton Street
Madison Wisconsin 53703
608.257.8400 FON
608.257.8440 FAX

162 Ravenhill Road
Orinda California 94563
510.254.4975 FON·FAX

IRONWOOD

Landscape Architecture
& Planning
P.O. Box 25
11452 Highway 62
Suite 255
Charlestown, IN 47111
Tel: (812) 284-7754
Fax: (812) 284-7970
Mobile: (502) 552-7777
E-mail: dabryan @ aol.com

David A. Bryan
Vice President

IRONWOOD

Client   Ironwood
              Charlestown, Indiana
Design Firm   Walter McCord & Mary Cawein Graphic Design
              Louisville, Kentucky

Contour graphed landscape is the artwork used on this card for landscape architects.
The name logo uses nice type relationships. Back of card is printed full bleed with
metallic ink; type is reversed.

Client   Time-Warner
              San Francisco, California
              New York, New York
Design Firm   Tharp Did It
              Los Gatos, California

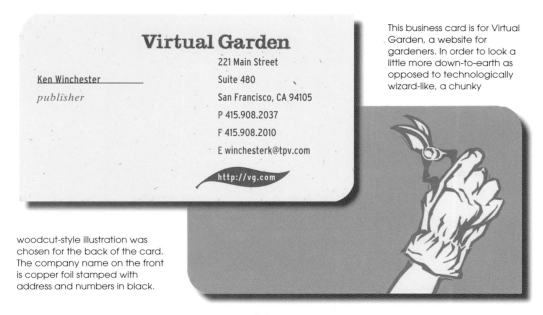

Virtual Garden

Ken Winchester

publisher

221 Main Street

Suite 480

San Francisco, CA 94105

P 415.908.2037

F 415.908.2010

E winchesterk@tpv.com

http://vg.com

This business card is for Virtual
Garden, a website for
gardeners. In order to look a
little more down-to-earth as
opposed to technologically
wizard-like, a chunky

woodcut-style illustration was
chosen for the back of the card.
The company name on the front
is copper foil stamped with
address and numbers in black.

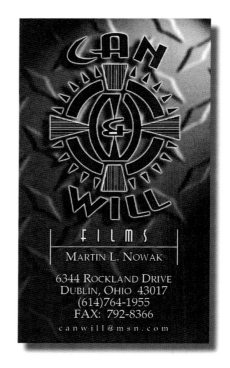

Client   Can & Will
              Dublin, Ohio
Design Firm   Rickabaugh Graphics
              Gahanna, Ohio

Printed in black and white, this card is for an independent film production company. Patterned metallic background and striking logo are strong graphic elements.

Client   Auburn Performing Arts Center
              Auburn, Washington
Design Firm   Art O Mat Design
              Seattle, Washington

Logo comprised of theater's initials in different type styles on loosely structured background blocks hints at an expressiveness encouraged by the cardholding entity. Yellow, red, and black are an attention-getting color scheme.

Client   Hot Rod Hell
              San Diego, California
Design Firm   Mires Design, Inc.
              San Diego, California

Wicked speed is indicated by the use of hot colors and flames.
You don't need the business name to tell you. Even if you love
working on cars, it can still sometimes be...a real trial.

Client   Rickabaugh Graphics
              Gahanna, Ohio
Design Firm   Rickabaugh Graphics
              Gahanna, Ohio

Very interesting background pattern, it seems tribal, full of figures,
symbols, or maybe nothing at all. Die cut business card has two
inverted corners.

Mark
Grennan

Multimedia
Designer

4747 Morena Boulevard, Suite 302
San Diego, California 92117
email: mark_grennan@fusionmedia.com
http://www.fusionmedia.com
telephone 619 490 5184
fax 619 490 5185

Client   Fusion Media
             San Diego, California
Design Firm Mires Design, Inc.
             San Diego, California

Oval business card printed in primary colors is outlined in silver metallic ink on one side. Silver ink is used as a background color on the other, leaving a white-edged border. Ovals of color intersect to relate the fusion idea.

Client   Phillip Marvin
             Eugene, Oregon
Design Firm Lincoln Design
             Eugene, Oregon

StrikeFore is a business of batting cages and a golf driving range. Teaching professional's business card doubles as an appointment card when the blank on the back is used. Baseball and golf icons are integrated into the company name to create an easy-to-remember logo.

JOE DANIELS, M.S.
Teaching Professional

STRIKE FORE

Batting Cages & Golf Driving Range

4501 W.11th Ave. & Beltline Rd., Eugene, OR 97402 • Ph. 485-7700

Client   NuTryx
            San Francisco, California
Design Firm Tharp Did It
            Los Gatos, California

Company that trains senior citizens to use the Internet shows a line drawing of an old dog suspiciously eyeing a computer on its business card. The back is covered with a pattern of "who says?" in typewriter font.

Client   Shimokochi/Reeves
            Los Angeles, California
Design Firm Shimokochi/Reeves
            Los Angeles, California

Bright blue and yellow are a very noticeable pair of colors. Blue lightning bolt is held aloft by a figure obviously strong enough to dominate it.

Client   Boelts Bros.,
                 Associates
            Tucson, Arizona
Design Firm Boelts Bros.,
                 Associates
            Tucson, Arizona

bba@boelts-bros.com

520.792.1026

FX 520.792.9720

345 EAST **UNIVERSITY** BOULEVARD • **TUCSON** • AZ • 85705•7848 • USA

BOELTS BROS. ASSOCIATES

NINA MAX DALY

520.792.1026

BOELTS BROS. ASSOCIATES

bba@boelts-bros.com

520.792.1026

FX 520.792.9720

345 EAST **UNIVERSITY** BOULEVARD • **TUCSON** • AZ • 85705•7848 • USA

BOELTS BROS. ASSOCIATES

JACKSON BOELTS

520.792.1026

BOELTS BROS. ASSOCIATES

jackson@boelts-bros.com

520.792.1026

FX 520.792.9720

345 EAST **UNIVERSITY** BOULEVARD • **TUCSON** • AZ • 85705•7848 • USA

BOELTS BROS. ASSOCIATES

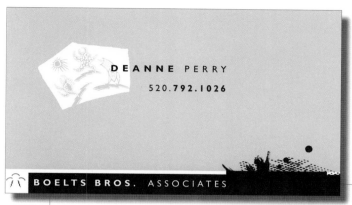

DEANNE PERRY
520.792.1026

🖐 **BOELTS BROS.** ASSOCIATES

This series of business cards for a design firm employs primitive icons, strong colors (printed negatively and positively), splashes, scribbles, and dollops. Each card has different images as do most fronts and backs of individual cards.

kerry@boelts-bros.com

520.**792.1026**

FX 520.792.9720

345 EAST UNIVERSITY BOULEVARD • **TUCSON** • AZ • **85705•7848** • USA

🖐 **BOELTS BROS.** ASSOCIATES

KERRY STRATFORD
520.**792.1026**

🖐 **BOELTS BROS.** ASSOCIATES

eric@boelts-bros.com

520.**792.1026**

FX 520.792.9720

345 EAST UNIVERSITY BOULEVARD • **TUCSON** • AZ • **85705•7848** • USA

🖐 **BOELTS BROS.** ASSOCIATES

ERIC BOELTS
520.**792.1026**

🖐 **BOELTS BROS.** ASSOCIATES

Client   OmniMedia
             Phoenix, Arizona
Design Firm After Hours Creative
             Phoenix, Arizona

Forties/fifties-style clip art images are used on this very modern, media marketer's card. Good image of "opening minds everywhere".

Client   STINKWEEDS
             Kimber Lanning
             Tempe, Arizona
Design Firm Harry3
             Muse Design
             Santa Fe,
                   New Mexico

Very fifties, but in "living color", business card for an indies record store is printed in color on one side, black and white on the other. One side is the company name integrated into a collection of iconography, while the flip offers more detailed information amidst some clip artish pics.

Client	Art O Mat Design
	Seattle, Washington
Design Firm	Art O Mat Design
	Seattle, Washington

Three different cards are printed in similar colors for a firm that specializes in design and marketing for commerce and the arts. For even more consistency, they are all designed with a flavor of the same era.

Client   Toll-Free Cellular
             Seattle, Washington
Design Firm Hornall Anderson Design Works
             Seattle, Washington

Subtle arc from corner to corner is printed behind the text on front of
business card. Technique is repeated on the back in different shades of
black. Good choice of green ink is easily readable on both light and
black surfaces.

Client   Pamela Kelly
             Los Angeles, California
Design Firm Shimokochi/Reeves
             Los Angeles, California

Communications consultant's business card displays an elliptical orbit
around her name and title. Nice change of color when the spheres cross
the purple bar.

jay harris

315 public square

troy, ohio 45373

v 937.335.9000

f 937.335.9001

e macman24@aol.com

i www.1–eg.com

design ✠ interactive solutions

Client   1-earth GRAPHICS
              Troy, Ohio
Design Firm   1-earth GRAPHICS
              Troy, Ohio

Celtic cross and typographic solutions with a slight medieval feel are a surprising success when combined with the logo's more modern approach to design. Unusual dimensions 1-5/8" x 3-5/8" add to this design firm's identity, as does the textured card stock.

Client   Andon Unlimited
              Renton, Washington
Design Firm   Gable Design Group
              Seattle, Washington

Graphics that indicate progression are nicely executed on this business card for the Tradeshow division of Wizards of the Coast. Spirals and orbs interact to create a sense of dimension with the aid of gradients and perspective.

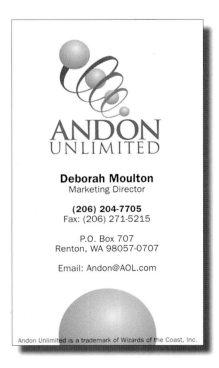

ANDON
UNLIMITED

Deborah Moulton
Marketing Director

(206) 204-7705
Fax: (206) 271-5215

P.O. Box 707
Renton, WA 98057-0707

Email: Andon@AOL.com

Andon Unlimited is a trademark of Wizards of the Coast, Inc.

Client   Best Cellars
          New York, New York
Design Firm Hornall Anderson Design Works
          Seattle, Washington

By the look of the purplish ring, it appears someone left a glass or bottle of wine setting on this business card for a wine retailer and distributor.

Client   Quail Crossing
          Boonville, Indiana
Design Firm Gregory R. Farmer
          Evansville, Indiana

A pattern of golf tees makes a border on one edge of this business card for a golf community. Effective typographic solutions include a quail drawing representing a "Q", and a golf ball for the dot on the "i".

Client   Tracy Nichols
                      Bonzi
                   San Francisco,
                      California
                   Italy

Design Firm   A E R I A L
                   San Francisco,
                   California

Metallic inks and vellum stock combine with beautiful art to create a really special series. Writing imagery was chosen for these cards for a writer who lives abroad. The vellum stock contributes to a great watermark effect, being able to see through to the printing from the other side.

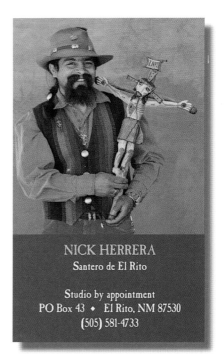

NICK HERRERA
Santero de El Rito

Studio by appointment
PO Box 43 ◆ El Rito, NM 87530
(505) 581-4733

Client   Nick Herrera
              Santa Fe, New Mexico
Design Firm   Cisneros Design
              Santa Fe, New Mexico

When the cardholder himself is as interesting as any graphic image,
why not use a photograph of him on his business card? In this case,
the artist holds a sample of his work so the viewer has an idea of
the style of art.

Client   Vantage Insurance Group
              Lancaster, Pennsylvania
Design Firm   Dean Design/Marketing Group, Inc.
              Lancaster, Pennsylvania

Corporate-looking, but out of the ordinary, business card repeats a
diamond shape alone and in accordance with the logo. Copper foil
stamping works nicely with navy ink. Notice the consistent use of flush right
type.

VANTAGE
INSURANCE
GROUP

ANDREA L. ROHRER
VICE PRESIDENT,
MARKETING

STERLING CENTER
SUITE 32-C
EAST ROSEVILLE ROAD
LANCASTER, PA 17601

PHONE 717-560-3030
FAX 717-560-2900
PA WATS 1-800-582-2855

Client   Suburban Construction, Inc.
             Madison, Wisconsin
Design Firm Z•D Studios, Inc.
             Madison, Wisconsin

Logo of this construction firm has a blueprint feel. Continuation of
angled line in logo is found above the text section of the card.

Client   Leveraged Learning
             Madison, Wisconsin
Design Firm Z•D Studios, Inc.
             Madison, Wisconsin

A globe on a seesaw-looking lever is the logo for this continuing educa-
tion association. Both images work well together even though the lever is
an illustration, and the globe appears to be a photograph.

University Village QFC
2746 NE 45th St.
Seattle, Washington 98105

TEL: 206.525.1200

Client   **Vivo**
           Seattle, Washington
Design Firm Gable Design Group
           Seattle, Washington

The logo of this gelateria incorporates one of the offered confections into the typography. Softer-than-primary colors are indicative of the frozen treats.

Client   **California Center for the Arts**
           Escondido, California
Design Firm Mires Design, Inc.
           San Diego, California

Typographic logo is printed on one side of this business card for a multi-disciplinary art center. The other side is printed full bleed yellow with type in black.

Neill Archer Roan

Executive Vice President

120 West Grand Avenue

Suite 105

Escondido, California

92025

Phone 619 738 4138

Fax 619 739 0205

Plant Address:
4918 20th Street East
Fife, WA 98424

Internet: michelle@quebim.com

Client   Quebecor
          Integrated Media
Tacoma,
          Washington
Design Firm Hornall Anderson
          Design Works, Inc.
Seattle,
          Washington

Reversed type, two-sided printing,
screened color, and repetition of
graphic elements all combine to
make a visually interesting card
series for an offset printer that
provides a full-range of services.

Client   Allo Spiedo & Brasserie Deitrich's
              Louisville, Kentucky
Design Firm   Walter McCord & Mary Cawein
                        Graphic Design
             Louisville, Kentucky

One folding business card is used for two different eateries, an Italian rosticceria and a French restaurant. Layouts are similar on both outsides of card with black bars and original artwork. Inside of card devotes equal space to each restaurant with descriptive phrases, addresses, and numbers.

ITALIAN CAFE

ALLO SPIEDO

ALLO SPIEDO ITALIAN CAFE

TUSCAN ROTISSERIED MEATS

WOOD OVEN PIZZA

ITALIAN WINE
& ESPRESSO BAR

ALFRESCO DINING UNDER
WISTERIA COVERED ARBOR

IN HISTORIC CRESCENT HILL

2309 FRANKFORT AVENUE
LOUISVILLE, KY 40206
(502) 895-4878

DEITRICH'S BRASSERIE

MODERN AMERICAN
& FRENCH CUISINE

LOCATED IN THE
CRESCENT THEATRE
(BUILT 1927)

ANTIQUE MAHOGANY BAR

SIDEWALK CAFÉ

HISTORIC CRESCENT HILL

2562 FRANKFORT AVENUE
LOUISVILLE, KY 40206
(502) 897-6076

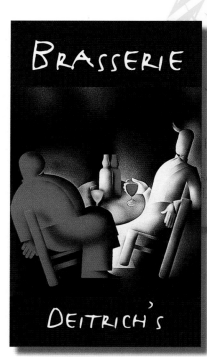

BRASSERIE

DEITRICH'S

Harry MacDonald Forehand III
328 North Park Ave.
Tucson, AZ 85719
60.26.23.33.57

Client   Harry MacDonald Forehand III
              Santa Fe, New Mexico
Design Firm   Harry3
              Muse Design
              Santa Fe, New Mexico

Ethereal business card uses only two colors in its printing. Red is printed full bleed and screened for maximum color options.

RICK WAS BORN IN 1952 IN MANSFIELD, OHIO.
HEN HE WENT TO COLLEGE AT MIAMI UNIVERSI
NOT IN FLORIDA). AND AFTER THAT HE CAME
ALIFORNIA AND OPENED A SMALL DESIGN STUD
CALLED THARP DID IT. HE NOW HAS FIVE OR
IX OTHERS DOING IT WITH HIM. SOMETIMES T
WIN AWARDS CERTIFICATES FOR THE STUFF THE
DO, (USUALLY NOT ON A COMPUTER), AND HAN
HEM ON A CLOTHESLINE ACROSS THE STUDIO.
WON A CLIO ONCE, BUT CAN'T FIND IT. RICK
IKES TO DO NON-CORPORATE IDENTITY, PACKA
ND POSTERS THAT GET INTO THE SMITHSONIAN
E U.S. LIBRARY OF CONGRESS. BIG DEAL YOU SAY?
HE CAN DO OTHER STUFF TOO. LIKE SKI, IRON
HIRTS AND TYPE. HE DISLIKES WHINERS, UPC
BAR CODES AND MOST SOFTWARE PROGRAMS EXCE
OR A COUPLE OF EASY ONES. H
AS ANOTHER OFFICE IN PORTL
REGON WITH A CREATIVE DIREC
RIEND. HE DOESN'T HAVE ANY
KIDS THAT HE KNOWS OF. THIS
AS PRINTED BY WATERMARK PRE

THARP

Client   Tharp Did It
              San Francisco, California
Design Firm   Tharp Did It
              Los Gatos, California

Front of card shows firm owner with his cross to bear and maybe not dealing with it quite as gracefully as the original Sacrifice. Personal information on back of business card reads like a dating service bio—very entertaining.

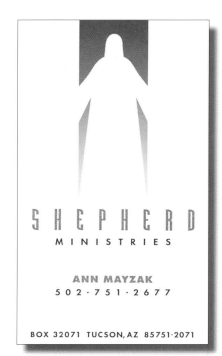

Client   Shepherd Ministries
            Tucson, Arizona
Design Firm Bartels & Company, Inc.
            St. Louis, Missouri

Bright white stock, metallic ink, and blue softened by gradation play an integral part in this card's design. Created for a prison ministry, the logo is a silhouette of an open-armed Jesus reversed out of blue.

Client   Disegno
            Mentor, Ohio
Design Firm Disegno
            Mentor, Ohio

A primary color scheme was chosen for this business card of a graphic design firm. Initial cap in the logo softens the reversed sans serif type in the remainder. Part of an ancient map is printed with a three-sided bleed on both front and back of card.

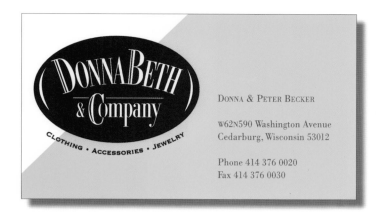

Client   Donna Beth & Company
              Cedarburg, Wisconsin
Design Firm   Becker Design
              Milwaukee, Wisconsin

Bright colors and unusual angles make a very vibrant, vital card that
indicates a fun and upbeat inventory from this clothing retailer.

Client   American Music Theatre
              Lancaster, Pennsylvania
Design Firm   Dean Design/Marketing Group
              Lancaster, Pennsylvania

A very clean-looking card uses purple, blue, and yellow inks for this
musical revue theater that produces original and classical shows.
Excellent shapes relationship between the musical note and star artwork.

Client   Rae Wilson
                Attleboro, Massachusetts
Design Firm   Adkins/Balchunas
                Pawtucket, Rhode Island

An idea that can function as a money saver while encouraging a
personal touch to every business card is a blank line on which any
employee's name can be handwritten—or dates, or sales…

Client   Gary's Hot Rods
                San Diego, California
Design Firm   Mires Design, Inc.
                San Diego, California

Repetition of flames makes sure the viewer gets the **hot** rod idea. Check
out the boss ride driving right out of the logo—really cherry!

Client **Buena Vista College**
Storm Lake, Iowa
Design Firm Sayles Graphic Design
Des Moines, Iowa

Strong logo of interlocked initials is used on business cards printed in both horizontal and vertical formats. One of the earthy tones from the logo is repeated in a border around all four edges of card front and back.

Client   Sophia McCrocklin
            Alexandria, Virginia
Design Firm Walter McCord & Mary
            Cawein Graphic Design
            Louisville, Kentucky

Extra large business card for a fiber artist
appropriately is printed on a fibered stock. Ink
matches perfectly.

SOPHIA M. **Mc**CROCKLIN
studio 14
Torpedo Factory
Art Center
105 N. Union Street
Alexandria (VA) 22314
phone
703 836-5807

Client   Dennis Hayes & Associates
            New York, New York
Design Firm Sagmeister Inc.
            New York, New York

Initial logo is constructed of squares of color for this post-production,
editing company. Even though the name includes "& associates", notice
that the figure stands alone.

DENNIS
HAYES
&
associates
incorporated

305 East 46 Street New York NY 10017-3058
telephone 212 980 0300 fax 212 755 1737

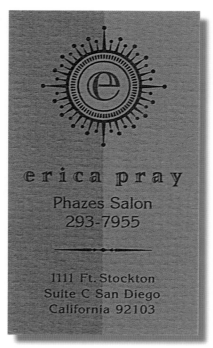

Client	Erica Pray
	San Diego, California
Design Firm	Billy Goats Gruff
	Encinitas, California

Business card series for a hair stylist includes not only different colors of stock, but different kinds of stock. Two colors of ink remain constant even to the point of what is printed with which: maroon is used for text, violet for art.

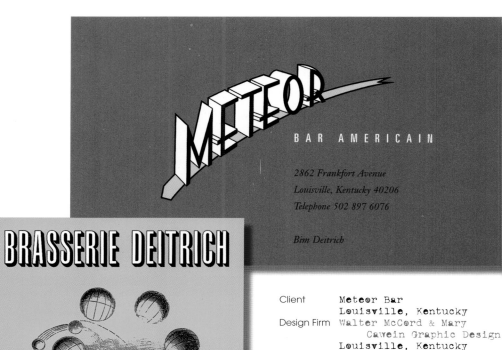

MÉTÉOR

BAR AMERICAIN

2862 Frankfort Avenue
Louisville, Kentucky 40206
Telephone 502 897 6076

Bim Deitrich

BRASSERIE DEITRICH

2862 FRANKFORT AVENUE   LOUISVILLE, KY 40206   TELEPHONE 502 897 6076

Client   Meteor Bar
               Louisville, Kentucky
Design Firm   Walter McCord & Mary
               Cawein Graphic Design
               Louisville, Kentucky
Illustrator   Dale Hoffman

Printed on both sides, this large business card has celestial images in reference to the name of the restaurant and bar.

Client   Comunica
               Santa Fe,
               New Mexico
Design Firm   Cisneros
               Design
               Santa Fe,
               New Mexico

Name in rough typewriter font boasts the only element on this card that's not in gray, the red dot above the "i".

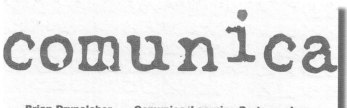

comunica

Brian Drypolcher   **Comunica/Learning Partners, Inc.**
                         1204 San José Avenue
                         Santa Fe, New Mexico 87505
                         505.820.7651
                         fax 505.982.7353
                         email comunica@trail.com

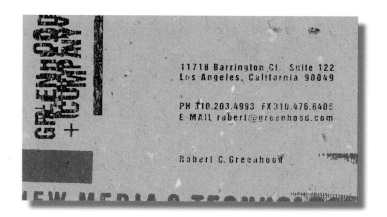

Client   Robert Greenhood/Greenhood & Company
                Los Angeles, California
Design Firm   Vrontikis Design Office
                Los Angeles, California

Grunge influenced card is rough-inked, rough-edged, and rough-stocked.
It's a design of its time and a good choice for new media consultants.

Client   Anne Meacham
                Des Moines, Iowa
Design Firm   Sayles Graphic Design
                Des Moines, Iowa

Printed in one color on front and back, a strong identity is affirmed by the
use of red ink only. All necessary information of this freelance creative
service is incorporated with art and type graphics in a pleasing format.

Client   Crafton Pease
              Atlanta, Georgia
Design Firm   Creative Soup, Inc.
              Atlanta, Georgia

Photographic representations of very different images are printed at the top of this card for a creative services firm. Type is reversed out of photos leading the viewer's eye down the card and into the main text section.

Client   NextLink Corporation
              Bellevue, Washington
Design Firm   Hornall Anderson Design Works, Inc.
              Seattle, Washington

Very interesting, but subtle, texture of light and shadow in the letters of the logo is repeated and printed full bleed on the back of card.

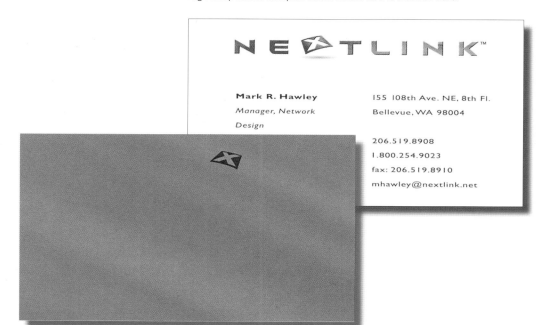

Client   Ralph McGrath
              Foster, Rhode Island
Design Firm   Adkins/Balchunas
              Pawtucket, Rhode Island

Great woodcut of a hand sawing wood (get it?) is the artwork for this business card of a custom carpenter.

Client   Doneckers
              Ephrata,
                 Pennsylvania
Design Firm   Dean Design/
              Marketing Group,
                            Inc.
              Lancaster,
                 Pennsylvania

Folded business card is a nice representation of upscale shopping, dining and a guesthouse complex. On the cover is a welcoming basket of fruit. Inside are found descriptions of different businesses, while the back has a map of the complex.

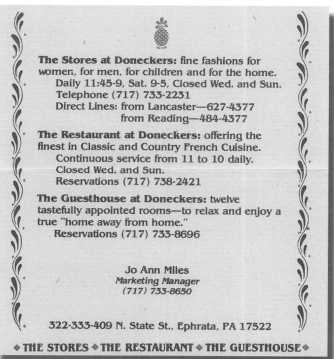

EXCELLEN

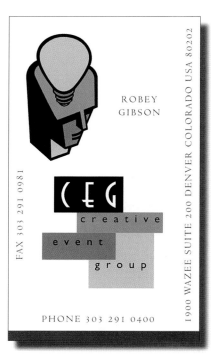

Client   CEG
              Creative Event Group
              Denver, Colorado
Design Firm   Ellen Bruss design
              Denver, Colorado

A different twist on the light bulb/idea genre, the graphics are
boxy to the point of flirting with cubism. Interesting shades of blue,
green, and brown make a memorable card for this group that
deals with large music festivals and concerts.

Client   Kevin Akers
              San Rafael, California
Design Firm   Kevin Akers
              San Rafael, California

Freely executed line drawings are printed on half of the front of this card
and full bleed on the back. Nice caricatures and characters give
meaning to the tag line "Design with Personality".

Client   Christner, Inc.
              St. Louis, Missouri
Design Firm   Bartels & Company, Inc.
              St. Louis, Missouri

Relationships between geometric shapes adorn this card for an architectural firm. Nice colors and good repetition of lines make this business card much more noticeable than the average.

Client   Homeworks
              Clive, Iowa
Design Firm   Sayles Graphic Design
              Des Moines, Iowa

Business card for a construction management company not only features a blueprint behind the house on the front, but part of an actual blueprint is printed full bleed on the back.

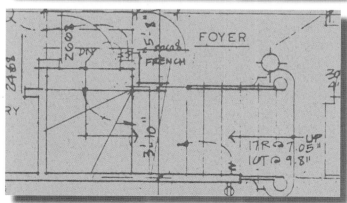

FAR OUT

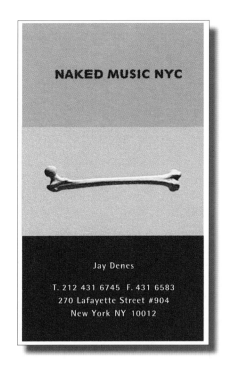

Client   Naked Music NYC
            New York, New York
Design Firm Sagmeister Inc.
            New York, New York

You can't get much more naked than this. Metallic silver ink was used as a surround color for the bone.

Client   Axiom
            Louisville, Kentucky
Design Firm Walter McCord
                    Graphic Design
            Louisville, Kentucky

Very cleanly designed cards use objects and different fonts in rebus-like logos for photographers. Notice that vertical and horizontal cards don't have the same logo.

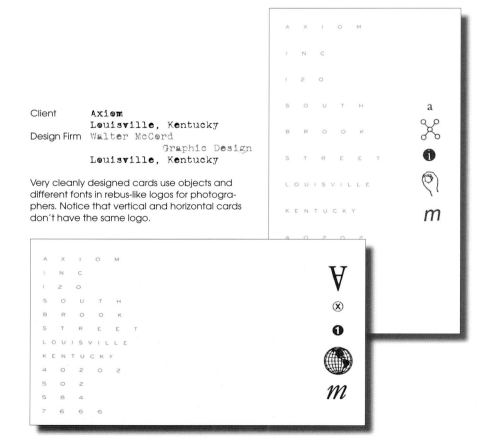

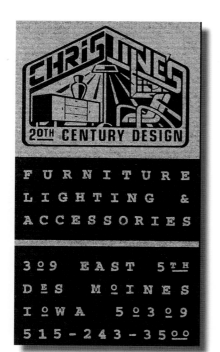

Client   Christine's
             Des Moines, Iowa
Design Firm Sayles Graphic Design
             Des Moines, Iowa

Black stock is the base for silver ink on this business card. The color effect works well for an antique shop that specializes in 20th century design.

Client   DHA (USA)
             New York, New York
Design Firm Sagmeister Inc.
             New York, New York

Photographic card for a consulting firm seems to indicate honesty and individuality.

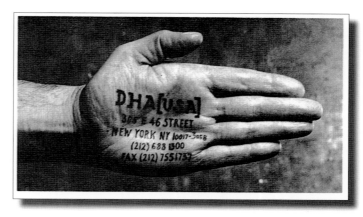

149

Client   Elena & Harry Forehand
             Santa Fe, New Mexico
Design Firm Harry3
             Muse Design
             Santa Fe, New Mexico

An updated version of a courtesy from days gone by
is the personal calling card. This one has an air of
mystery with surreal images on the front and fantasy
characters on the back all done in gentle and dark
shades.

Client   Bartels & Company, Inc.
             St. Louis, Missouri
Design Firm Bartels & Company, Inc.
             St. Louis, Missouri

A blue tiger jumping through a hoop of fire seems a rather tongue-in-
cheek logo for an advertising design agency. Round line of the hoop is
repeated in the typography encircling the logo.

Client   Lazarus
              Des Moines, Iowa
Design Firm   Sayles Graphic Design
              Des Moines, Iowa

Business consultants' card focuses more on the name "Lazarus" than the actual service offered. With a butterfly-like figure in the background of a boxed-in Lazarus, one can't help but see symbolism of "Lazarus Being Raised from the Dead". Butterflies are symbols of life and rebirth, and in this case the symbol overshadows the "entombed" Lazarus.

Client   Aurea
              Scotts Valley,
                  California
Design Firm   Kevin Akers
              San Rafael,
                  California

Headset manufacturer's business card has all text except the cardholder's name printed in purple ink. (The name is printed in black.) Purple is repeated full bleed on the back. Metallic gold orbit from the logo is repeated on the back in the form an ellipse.

JOSEPH J. VITUG
Engineering Product Manager

ACS WIRELESS, INC
10 VICTOR SQUARE
SCOTTS VALLEY
CALIFORNIA 95066
408/438-3883 ext.4239
Fax 408/438-7730
jvitug@acs.com

AUREA™

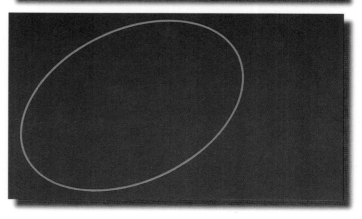

CONRAD'S
BAR & GRILL

MARK FOX

326 West Jericho Turnpike
Huntington, New York 11743
516.427.9728   516.427.9751

Client   Conrad's
            Huntington, New York
Design Firm Adkins/Balchunas
            Pawtucket, Rhode Island

A dark, handsome stranger is included in the illustrative logo of this
bar & grill. Line-textured stock adds visual interest.

Client   BVP Media, Inc.
            Englewood, Colorado
Design Firm Ellen Bruss design
            Denver, Colorado

Body parts representative of our senses were chosen to be the art on this
card for a company that deals with video and film, and whose tag line
reads "come to your senses". This card is printed on both sides with each
sense in a different media.

Chef Claus

CLAUS PW BIENEK

Work 414 359 3731
Home 414 238 1298

Client   Chef Claus
            Milwaukee, Wisconsin
Design Firm Becker Design
            Milwaukee, Wisconsin

Cleanly designed business card suggests elegance and simplicity through font and color choices, and checkered border.

Client   Brian Meredith
            Oceanside, California
Design Firm Mires Design, Inc.
            San Diego, California

Indicating a mastery of the English language, an archetypal English gentleman employs a fountain pen for his cane. Oversized business card is sure to get noticed, and the tag line "Jolly Good Copy" is quite a pleasant phrase.

BRIAN MEREDITH
≡ SPECIALIZING IN ≡
Jolly Good Copy

2051 GENEVA STREET № 54 OCEANSIDE CALIFORNIA 92054
telephone 619-754-0373 fax 619-757-5453

Client   Companion Baking Company
                 St. Louis, Missouri
Design Firm   Bartels & Company, Inc.
                 St. Louis, Missouri

Baking-indicative shades of brown are a clue that this business card is for a baker of hand crafted bread. Informal typography further adds to the tone of comfort.

Client   Turner & Martin
                 Palo Alto, California
Design Firm   Russell Leong Design
                 Palo Alto, California

Certainly all the information on this oversized card could have fit on one of regular size, but the effect would have suffered. Printed in two colors, this card positively maximizes the use of white space.

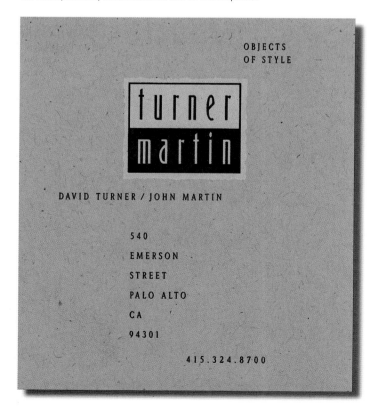

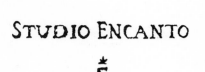

STUDIO ENCANTO

É.

CHRISTY MARTIN

STUDIO ENCANTO INCORPORATED
6262 No. SWAN ROAD, SUITE 100 TUCSON, AZ 85718 USA
TEL. 520.615.9441 FAX 520.615.0441

Scala de Piedi vincic.

Client   Studio Encanto
           Tucson, Arizona
Design Firm Boelts Bros., Associates
           Tucson, Arizona

Short card for an Italian inspired interior design firm has a very hands-on
feel with typography and lines that look drawn. Notice the slight color
difference in the border from the front of the card and the background
from the back.

Client   Consolidated
           Management Co.
           Des Moines, Iowa
Design Firm Sayles Graphic
                   Design
           Des Moines, Iowa

Hungry Camper is a camp food
service. The business card employs
many camp graphics and some
hand-lettered type for a fun,
informal image.

A DIVISION OF CONSOLIDATED MANAGEMENT CO.

H U N G R Y

2894 106TH STREET SUITE 104

DES MOINES, IOWA 50322

(515) 278-9774

FAX (515) 254-0394

RICK W. LEVI
PRESIDENT

C A M P E R

Client   Hornall Anderson Design Works, Inc.
            Seattle, Washington
Design Firm Hornall Anderson Design Works, Inc.
            Seattle, Washington

Series of business cards for a graphic design firm differ in color only. One of two versions of the logo is printed on the front and back of business card, respectively. The intersection of the firm's initial inside a conical image is an interesting representation. One version is a line drawing which offers more chance for optical-illusion effects. The other is printed in a more solid, three-dimensional manner. Three-sided bleed, color printing is flipped oppositely from one side to the other.

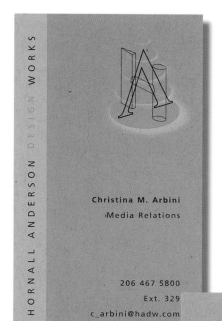

HORNALL ANDERSON DESIGN WORKS

Christina M. Arbini
Media Relations

206 467 5800
Ext. 329
c_arbini@hadw.com

HORNALL ANDERSON DESIGN WORKS

1008
Western Ave
Suite 600
Seattle, WA
98104

206 467 5800
FAX 467 6411
www.hadw.com

HORNALL ANDERSON DESIGN WORKS

Christina M. Arbini
Media Relations

206 467 5800
Ext. 329
c_arbini@hadw.com

Client **La Terraza**
Pennington, New Jersey
Design Firm Main Street Design
Pennington, New Jersey

Home and garden accessories from Latin America are exemplified in nice line drawings highlighted by color washes. Rough-textured card stock complements artwork well.

LA TERRAZA

Garden Appointments
and Home Accessories
From Latin America

GRETCHEN CHRISTIE

276 North Main Street
Pennington, New Jersey 08534
609•730•4255

LA TERRAZA

Garden Appointments
and Home Accessories
From Latin America

GRETCHEN CHRISTIE

276 North Main Street
Pennington, New Jersey 08534
609•730•4255

LA TERRAZA

Garden Appointments
and Home Accessories
From Latin America

GRETCHEN CHRISTIE

276 North Main Street
Pennington, New Jersey 08534
609•730•4255

Client   Hoffmann & Angelic Design
             White Rock, British Columbia, Canada
Design Firm Hoffmann & Angelic Design
             White Rock, British Columbia, Canada

Sweeping lines and beautifully rendered, handlettered type are examples of this design firm's work available for viewing right on their business card.

Client   Flora
             Arlington, Massachusetts
Design Firm Fyfe Design
             Cambridge, Massachusetts

Free-spirited card for a restaurant uses purple and peach. Fun drawings clearly state that this place serves good food and good times.

Client   Tosca
              Hingham, Massachusetts
Design Firm   Adkins/Balchunas
              Pawtucket, Rhode Island

Nice combination of colors combine for a subdued but individual-
ized effect. Card background is divided into halves. One is printed
with a brown maroon ink, while the other is a plaster/canvas
texture.

Client   Daphne Raider/Twist Salon
              Evansville, Indiana
Design Firm   Gregory R. Farmer Design
              Evansville, Indiana

Hair salon's card is printed with metallic ink and black thermog-
raphy on flecked black stock. The contour of the logo-esque
twist of hair is followed in name and shape by the name of the
salon.

Client   Corey Weiser
             Washington, D.C.
Design Firm Sheila Woodbridge
             Washington, D.C.

Unusually shaped and sized (2-1/4" x 2-1/4") business card
for an artist shows an example of her work. Printed on
heavy vellum, metallic ink image on the back of card
shows through to the front. The image is repeated in a
smaller version in the bottom right corner.

Client   Bradley Group, Inc.
             Los Angeles, California
Design Firm Margo Chase Design
             Los Angeles, California

Folded business card has a die cut flap printed full bleed black with only
two images. Opened, you find all the necessary information for the
Bradley Group which specializes in sales and support of Macintosh based
systems for design editing and post production.

213-465-7593

fax 213-465-7679

james bradley   B R A D L E Y group

6646 hollywood blvd #229

hollywood ca 90028

Client   Sheehan Design
              Seattle, Washington
Design Firm   Sheehan Design
              Seattle, Washington

Very '40s in style, this business card for a graphic design & advertising firm is quite eye-catching. Printed only in black (the red arrow appears rubber stamped) all elements point the viewer to the text area. A partial frame is created by lines on the left and bottom. The underline breaks the circle and guides the eye to "Studio". Of course the arrow points exactly where to go, and the figure at bottom right helps frame with his body while his fingers point to name and address.

Client   Pet Fair
              Tacoma, Washington
Design Firm   Sheehan Design
              Seattle, Washington

Pet Fair tradeshow has such successful images on its card, it hardly needs the name. A pet collar is printed across the top, bleeding left and right. Hooked onto the collar is a foil stamped tag that reads "Pet Fair".

BARBARA TABACH

Schaffer's Bridal and Formal Shop

Client   Schaffers Bridal Shop
            Des Moines, Iowa
Design Firm Sayles Graphic Design
            Des Moines, Iowa

Bridal and formal wear shop has two cards. For women a gowned female illustration is the icon; for men a tuxedo-clad lad is the picture. On the back of each card, in horizontal orientation, are found two addresses and the logo.

300 Eighth Street
(Corner of Eighth and Walnut)
Des Moines, Iowa 50309
515/288-0356 • FAX 243-0122

Schaffer's

Country Club Plaza
4626 JC Nichols Parkway
Kansas City, Missouri 64112
816/756-2027 • FAX 756-3904

BARNEY TABACH

Schaffer's Bridal and Formal Shop

Microsoft Corporation
One Microsoft Way
Redmond, WA 98052-6399

Tel 206 936 3831
Fax 206 936 7329
Telex 160520 Microsoft BVUE
Internet: hughc@microsoft.com

-my #

where I work

me!

Microsoft ®
kids & games unit

Hugh Chang
Lead Program Manager
Kids - HPU

Client   Microsoft Kids & Games Business Unit
         Redmond, Washington
Design Firm   Hansen Design Company
         Seattle, Washington

A boring card brightened immediately with a crayon influence!

Client   Gallery Trabant
         Portland, Oregon
Design Firm   Russell Leong Design
         Palo Alto, California

Logo is enlarged and printed in one color with a two-sided bleed on the
back of this card for an art gallery that specializes in designs from central/
eastern Europe.

Sharon A. Drummond

GALLERY ⑤ TRABANT

CONTEMPORARY DESIGNS FROM CENTRAL/EASTERN EUROPE

705 NW ELEVENTH AVENUE • PORTLAND, OR 97209
TEL 503.222.7411 • FAX 503.222.5510 • EMAIL TRABANTUSA@AOL.COM

JERRY COWART DESIGNERS, INC.

JERRY COWART
818.718.5981

22301 ACORN ST CHATSWORTH, CA 91311
FAX 818.718.5983   E-MAIL JCDEZINER@AOL.COM

Client   Jerry Cowart Designers
              Chatsworth, California
Design Firm   Jerry Cowart Designers
              Chatsworth, California

Do you really need an explanation of the art after you've seen the
designer's name?

Client   Strategic Change Management
              Phoenix, Arizona
Design Firm   After Hours Creative
              Phoenix, Arizona

Taking its cue from the company name, the art on this card features one
of the most strategic change artists in pop culture.

STRATEGIC CHANGE MANAGEMENT

SCOTT JACOBSON

4329 E. McDONALD PHOENIX, AZ 85018
PH 602 840-6509   FAX 602 840-7501
ScottJ01@aol.com

Client   Instinct
            Milwaukee, Wisconsin
Design Firm Becker Design
            Milwaukee, Wisconsin

Series of business cards for an art gallery are distinctive in not only shape, but also the painterly type used for the entity's name.

725 N.   Milwaukee St. Milw. WI 53202   414 **276-6363**

725 N. Milwaukee St.
Milw. WI 53202 414 **276-6363**

725 N. Milwaukee St. Milw. WI 53202   414 **276-6363**

725 N. Milwaukee St.
Milw. WI 53202
414 **276-6363**

Client   Mark & Laura Tindell
              Barford, England
Design Firm   Kevin Akers
              San Rafael, California

Personal calling card has a very homey look with house illustration and soft color choices for the background.

Client   Armin Schneider
              Austria
Design Firm   Sagmeister Inc.
              New York, New York

Laminated card for badminton devotee should be lit from behind to witness the entire game.

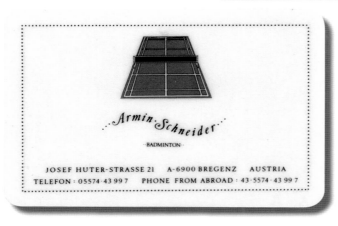

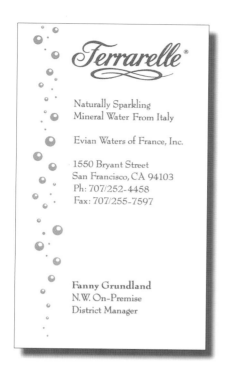

Ferrarelle®

Naturally Sparkling
Mineral Water From Italy

Evian Waters of France, Inc.

1550 Bryant Street
San Francisco, CA 94103
Ph: 707/252-4458
Fax: 707/255-7597

Fanny Grundland
N.W. On-Premise
District Manager

Client   Ferrarelle
            Italy
Design Firm Kevin Akers
            San Rafael, California

Delicately rising bubbles adorn this card for a seller of mineral water.

Client   Atherton
            New York, New York
            Los Angeles, California
Design Firm Margo Chase Design
            Los Angeles, California

This card for a commercial production company has a real circus flavor from the font chosen for the company name, to the dressed animals doing acrobatic tricks.

ATHERTON

elizabeth kinder
....
executive producer
beth@athertonny.com

49 east 21st street • third floor
new york, new york 10010
tel 212.473.4800
fax 212.473.1133
e-mail: info@athertonny.com

5440 hollywood blvd. • second floor
los angeles, california 90028
tel 213.957.8550
fax 213.957.8531
e-mail: info@athertonla.com

P.O. BOX 4290
NAPA, CA
94558

FAX: 707 255 0928
TEL: 707 255 2711

JO ANN WILLIAMSON
BUSINESS ADMINISTRATOR

Client   Areti Wines
            Napa, California
Design Firm Buttitta Design
            Healdsburg, California

Elegant card in wine and olive inks uses unobtrusive graphics to
complement typography, not overpower it.

Client   Tableaux
            Tokyo, Japan
Design Firm Vrontikis Design Office
            Los Angeles, California

Double-sided card for an upscale Japanese restaurant is exactly the
same on both sides except one is printed in English and the other in
Japanese.

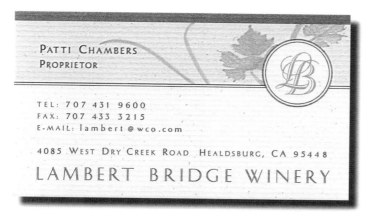

Client   **Lambert Bridge Winery**
            Healdsburg, California
Design Firm Buttitta Design
            Healdsburg, California

Grape leaves and intertwined initials are beautifully rendered elements for this lovely business card.

Client   **Innovative Stone**
            Houston, Texas
Design Firm Kelman Design Studio
            Houston, Texas

Folded business card is embossed on the covered with "chiseled" letters and a marble column. This company fabricates marble.

TRENDY

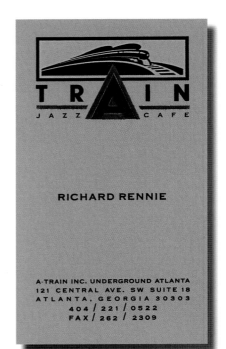

RICHARD RENNIE

A-TRAIN INC. UNDERGROUND ATLANTA
121 CENTRAL AVE. SW SUITE 18
ATLANTA, GEORGIA 30303
404 / 221 / 0522
FAX / 262 / 2309

Client   A Train
             Atlanta, Georgia
Design Firm Bartels & Company, Inc.
             St. Louis, Missouri

Jazz cafe's logo incorporates variegated foil stamping into the logo. Surrounding the "A" and underlining the remainder of the name, foil adds that something extra to an already nice card.

Client   The Finishing Touch
             Des Moines, Iowa
Design Firm Sayles Graphic Design
             Des Moines, Iowa

Business card for a finishing services and handwork company shows examples of some of what they offer: rubber stamping and three-dimensional add-ons. An unusually tactile card, you just want to keep touching it.

Client   Linx Technologies
            Woburn, Massachusetts
Design Firm Adkins/Balchunas
            Pawtucket, Rhode Island

Repetition of a lightning bolt indicates the energy of this telecommunications business. Complementary color scheme of yellow and purple forms a gradient behind the company name.

Client   Storyboards
            Venice, California
Design Firm Vrontikis Design Office
            Los Angles, California

Rough representation of a storyboard display also is reminiscent of a road, both indicating progression, change, moving forward—it's a good thing.

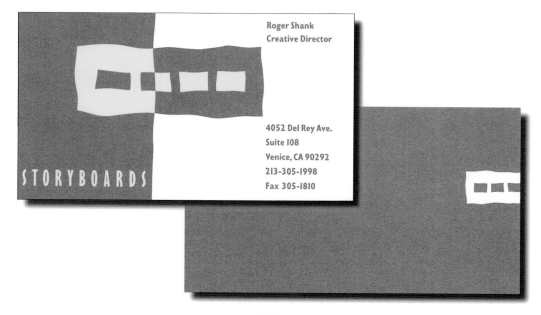

Client   Hyland Printing
             West Warwick, Rhode Island
Design Firm   Adkins/Balchunas
             Pawtucket, Rhode Island

This card has a nice mix of metallic and regular inks, screens and
solid colors. Great collage imagery of printing gears and stuff is
masterfully executed.

Client   Communiqué
             San Rafael, California
Design Firm   A E R I A L
             San Francisco, California

Phone receiver images are aided in representation by delicate hole
punching. This business card for a communications etiquette training
service uses bright orange red and gray for its palette.

Cindy M. Sonnenberg

Communiqué

1010 B Street
Suite 401
San Rafael
94901
415/457-6621

Communications
Etiquette
Training

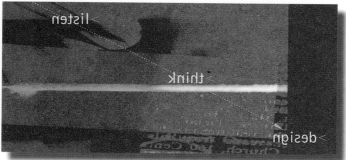

Client   Vrontikis Design Office
             Los Angeles, California
Design Firm Vrontikis Design Office
             Los Angeles, California

Blocks of color divide the front of this card into sections, but also interact
with each other by use of type that traverses the color chasm. On the
back is a dark collage. Reversed out of it in white is stated a succinct and
successful design process in relation to fulfilling the client's needs.

Client   Orts Theater of Dance
             Tucson, Arizona
Design Firm Boelts Bros., Associates
             Tucson, Arizona

Bright color and free use of typography give this card a sense of
movement and power.

K A R E

Karen Tyler

One-of
a-kind
Funwear

Post Office

Box 43546

Tucson, Arizona

8 5 7 3 3

602-326-7934

W E A R

Client   Kare Ware
            Tucson, Arizona
Design Firm Boelts Bros., Associates
            Tucson, Arizona

Soft colors, askew type, and playful figures set the tone of this
business card for a handmade children's clothing company.

Client   Otto
            Cambridge, Massachusetts
Design Firm Fyfe Design
            Cambridge, Massachusetts

Freely rendered drawing of a playful dog adorns this large
business card for a restaurant. Two cards were printed full bleed
on both sides with alternating colors.

otto

344 huron ave
cambridge
354.6699

Client   Timbuktuu Coffee Bar
             Des Moines, Iowa
Design Firm Sayles Graphic Design
             Des Moines, Iowa

Coffee beans and primitive art are used on this card (and the entire corporate identity). Logo is printed on one side and the necessary info on the other.

Client   Chaos Lures
             San Diego, California
Design Firm Mires Design, Inc.
             San Diego, California

Active art printed in color as the logo and monochromatically in the background is the highlight of this business card for a manufacturer of fishing lures. Knotted border adds to the fishing theme.

Client	Debra Folsom Design
	Telluride, Colorado
Design Firm	Barbara Raab Design
	Alexandria, Virginia

Interior designer's card uses muted greens and graceful architectural elements to represent its business.

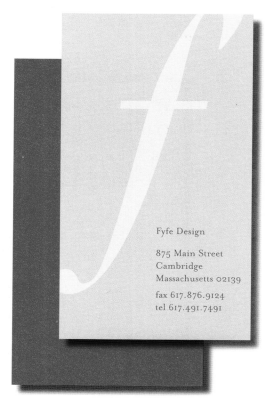

Client	Fyfe Design
	Cambridge, Massachusetts
Design Firm	Fyfe Design
	Cambridge, Massachusetts

Italic lowercase "f" is the main graphic on this card for a design firm. Type is printed in magenta against a celery background. Backside of card is full bleed magenta which indicates there are two sides to this firm's design.

R J MUNA

PICTURES

RAJA J. MUNA

225 INDUSTRIAL STREET
SAN FRANCISCO, CALIFORNIA
ZIP 94124-8975

415.468.8225 TEL
415.468.8295 FAX
pictures@rjmuna.com NET

Client   R J Muna
              San Francisco,
                      California
Design Firm   A E R I A L
              San Francisco,
                      California

Each card from this series has all
information printed on one side in black.
The other side is one of a variety of soft
focus halftones printed full bleed.

still | moving | pictures

still | moving | pictures

still | moving | pictures

still | moving | pictures

DAVID SALANITRO
principal

fax 415 834 9396

DSALANITRO@OHBOYCO.COM

NO.

415 834 9063

49 GEARY STREET, SUITE 530
SAN FRANCISCO, CALIFORNIA 94108

Graphic Design
OH BOY, A DESIGN COMPANY
Est. 1994

DAVID LEVISON
business development manager

fax 415 834 9396

DLEVISON@OHBOYCO.COM

NO.

415 834 9063

49 GEARY STREET, SUITE 530
SAN FRANCISCO, CALIFORNIA 94108

Graphic Design
OH BOY, A DESIGN COMPANY
Est. 1994

Client   Oh Boy, A Design Company
              San Francisco, California
Design Firm   Oh Boy, A Design Company
              San Francisco, California

Uniquely-shaped business cards for a graphic design firm look rather like tickets with even a tear-off section which includes the logo.

Client   1 Horsepower Design
              Los Alamos, New Mexico
Design Firm   1 Horsepower Design
              Los Alamos, New Mexico

"Fight visual pollution" is exemplified in not only the artwork on this card but in the overall design. Visual and mental images of power/strength are prevalent.

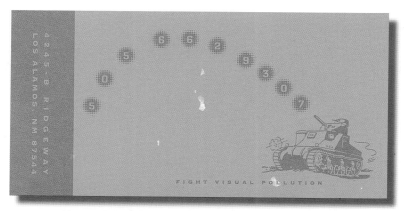

7134 Countrywood Lane
Madison WI 53719

voice 608.695.9283

page 608.559.9399

fax 608.845.8451

Client   Image Gate
             Madison, Wisconsin

Design Firm   Z•D Studios
             Madison, Wisconsin

Film production company's business card employes a die cut edge to frame the film strip on the card. Company name is on each cell of the strip.

Client   Steep & Brew
             Madison, Wisconsin

Design Firm   Z•D Studios
             Madison, Wisconsin

Folded business cards always create interest because the viewer must take an active part in acquiring the information.

Steep & Brew
Coffee Roasters

855 EAST BROADWAY
MADISON, WI 53716

TEL   608-223-0707
        800-876-1986
FAX   608-223-0355

KARI ALWIN
Business Manager

Client   1-earth GRAPHICS
             Troy, Ohio
Design Firm 1-earth GRAPHICS
             Troy, Ohio

Narrow business card employs only two-color printing, but on colored stock. Strong graphics and type printed in black are easily read.

Client   Hanzon Studios
             Denver, Colorado
Design Firm Ellen Bruss design
             Denver, Colorado

Handlettered scribbles are an incoherent, but great textured, background for this business card for a conceptual design studio. Logo is created with initials of company in two different fonts.

Index